30 minute CURRIES

30 minute CURRIES

contents

30 mins

All the recipes in the is book can be prepared in under 30 minutes. Some require ingredients which take a little longer to marinade or drain, but you can plan ahead to ensure these are ready-to-use when you commence cooking. Most of the curries will be cooked within 30 minutes too ensuring you have a tasty, authentic curry in the shortest possible time.

a world
of flavour

For such a humble sounding word, 'curry' refers to some of the world's most delicious and popular dishes. The word itself was first coined by the British in India, possibly deriving from the Tamil word kari, meaning 'spiced sauce'. Today the term covers dishes that range from simple to sophisticated, complex to singularly bold, those that can be made in minutes or left for hours over a bed of coals, and includes the everyday food of peasants to the once-exclusive creations of the rich and royal.

Use of the word has expanded to include the curries of Southeast Asia alongside those of India, and this book features dishes from cuisines as varied as those of Kashmir, Goa, Bangladesh, Thailand, Malaysia, Sri Lanka, Laos and Vietnam. Despite this diversity, all curries share a few essential elements: a curry paste, seasonings — which can vary from fresh herbs to pungent shrimp paste — and the 'main' ingredient, such as meat, fish, pulses or vegetables. From there, curries can go in many directions. They may be dry, oily, wet, thick or thin. The cooking can involve frying, boiling, steaming or slow, gentle braising. Adjectives such as sour, salty, hot, sweet, creamy, pungent and fragrant may all be applied to a finished dish, more often than not in combination. In fact, if anything unites curries, it is their skill in blending various tastes, textures and aromas to create superb dishes of great depth and balance.

The essential starting place is the curry paste. The paste will infuse the other ingredients with its flavour and fragrance, and its creation is a real part of the pleasure of making a curry. Traditionally, curry pastes are made by hand, the ingredients added one-by-one to a mortar for grinding or to the frying pan for roasting, with the cook observing, smelling and adjusting as necessary. Buying prepared spice mixtures is convenient, but to experience the real thing, have a go at preparing one from scratch.

Of course, the other thing that unites curries is rice. This staple of life is central to the cuisines of India and Southeast Asia, and curries are there to support the rice — not the other way round. Once again, the trick is to seek balance, combining delicately perfumed rice with vegetable dishes, side dishes and curries to match. This book contains some classic raitas, pickles and breads to experiment with and many more wonderful curries that amply demonstrate the delight to be found in this age-old dish.

The perfect rice

Anywhere there is curry, rice will be close to hand. Although there are three basic rice types available, only long-grain is considered the natural accompaniment to curries. Compared with short- and medium-grain rices, long-grain is generally thinner, longer, less starchy and when cooked yields a light fluffy, loose-grained texture. There are several varieties of long-grain rice and although, at a pinch, any will do the trick, for authenticity try serving the dry, separate grained, nutty-tasting basmati rice with Indian curries and aromatic, slightly clingy, floral scented jasmine rice alongside Thai curries. The flavours of both these rice varieties complement the spices in the curries from the corresponding cuisines.

Absorption method

Put the rice in a saucepan and shake so that it evenly coats the bottom of the pan. Stick the very tip of your finger into the rice then add enough cold water to come up to the first finger joint. Bring to the boil over high heat then cover with a clear, tight-fitting lid. Reduce heat to low and cook until the water has mostly evaporated and small steam holes appear on the surface of the rice. Remove the lid, fluff with a fork and serve.

Rapid boil method

Bring a large saucepan of water to the boil over high heat. Sprinkle over the rice and cook according to the instructions on the packet or until the grains are tender. Drain the rice in a colander. If using jasmine rice, which is slightly glutinous, rinse with a little tepid water before serving.

Three ways with rice

It is impossible to overestimate the importance of rice for the peoples of Southeast Asia and India. Indeed, curries are there to support the rice, not the other way around. Rice is combined with ingredients ranging from the most humble to the most luxurious. Saffron, the world's most expensive spice, is used to flavour Indian and Persian rice dishes, such as pilaff and biryani, while other staples such as lentils and coconut are also common, and delicious, additions to rice.

Saffron rice

SERVES 6 * PREPARATION TIME: 5 MINUTES + SOAKING TIME
COOKING TIME: 20 MINUTES

Wash 400 g (14 oz/2 cups) basmati rice, cover with cold water and soak for 30 minutes, then drain. Melt 25 g (1 oz) butter in a frying pan over medium heat then add 3 bay leaves and the drained rice. Cook, stirring, for 6 minutes, or until all the moisture has evaporated. Meanwhile, soak ¼ teaspoon saffron threads in 2 tablespoons hot water for a few minutes then add to the rice with 500 ml (17 fl oz/2 cups) boiling vegetable stock, 375 ml (13 fl oz/1½ cups) boiling water and salt to taste. Bring to the boil, then reduce the heat and cook, covered, for 12–15 minutes, or until all the water is absorbed and the rice is cooked.

Seasoned rice and lentils

SERVES 6 * PREPARATION TIME: 10 MINUTES * COOKING TIME: 25 MINUTES

Wash 300 g (10½ oz/1½ cups) basmati rice and 300 g (10½ oz/1⅔ cups) split mung beans (mung lentils) then drain and set aside. Heat 2 tablespoons oil in a frying pan, add 1 sliced onion, 3 bay leaves, 1 teaspoon cumin seeds, 2 pieces cassia bark, 1 tablespoon cardamom seeds, 6 cloves and ¼ teaspoon black peppercorns and cook over low heat for 5 minutes, or until the onion is softened and the spices are fragrant. Add the rice and lentils, and cook, stirring, for 2 minutes. Pour in 1.25 litres (44 fl oz/5 cups) water and salt to taste. Bring to the boil, then reduce the heat and cook, covered, over low heat for 15 minutes. Stir gently to avoid breaking the grains and cook, uncovered, over low heat for 3 minutes, or until all the moisture has evaporated. Discard the whole spices when the dish is cooked.

Coconut rice

SERVES 6 * PREPARATION TIME: 10 MINUTES
COOKING TIME: 12 MINUTES + SITTING TIME

Rinse 400 g (14 oz/2 cups) long-grain rice and cover with 1 litre (35 fl oz/4 cups) water. Set aside for 30 minutes then drain. Bring 750 ml (26 fl oz/3 cups) water to the boil. Add the rice, 1 pandanus leaf tied in a knot and salt to taste. Reduce the heat and cook, covered, for 12 minutes, or until the rice is just cooked. Remove from heat and add 185 ml (6 fl oz/¾ cup) coconut cream. Stir gently to avoid breaking the grains. Cover and set aside for 10 minutes, or until the rice absorbs the coconut cream in the residual heat. Discard the pandanus leaf before serving.

vegetarian curries

Vegetable curries are popular throughout India and Southeast Asia, due to the superb fresh produce available in these regions. Popular vegetables used in these curries are spinach, aubergine, squash, potatoes, lentils, mushrooms and tomatoes. The recipes that follow are a great representation of vegetable curries, for example the classic Indian dahl, the musaman vegetable curry, or the Indonesian squash and spinach curry.

Most curries could be described as aromatic, through their use of herbs and spices known primarily for their fragrant qualities. Pepper, chillies and turmeric are all aromatic, but that is not what first comes to mind when thinking about the impact they have on a curry. On the other hand, fresh Thai basil and coriander (cilantro) leaves, cloves and nutmeg all suggest dishes whose aroma — be it sweet, clean, sharp or pungent — immediately invites and seduces.

Thai cooking in particular makes good use of fresh herbs to engage the sense of smell. If Indian cooking excels at combining dried spices, Thai cooking delights in creating curries with layers of flavour and aroma from a wide range of fresh herbs, spices and seasonings. These include local ingredients such as the aniseed-like Thai basil, floral kaffir lime (makrut) leaves and tangy galangal, as well as more familiar ones such as coriander, ginger, lemon grass, garlic, spring onions (scallions) and onions. It is sometimes easy to overlook the importance of these reliable stalwarts, but few curries could do without the body and flavour they provide, as well as their sharp, clean and sweet aromas.

A Thai green curry is the classic example of this art, blending most of the above with vegetables, chicken or fish in a coconut-based sauce with green chillies for heat. The finished dish — tart, salty and hot — is generously garnished with fresh-tasting, fragrant makrut and Thai basil leaves. Thai curries are renowned for the care taken with the preparation and cooking of ingredients, and the frying of the curry paste is a careful exercise in letting your nose tell you when to add the next ingredient. Learning to recognize the different aromas of herbs and spices is not essential for the occasional curry cook — you'll still produce delicious results — but is certainly something dedicated lovers of curries aspire to.

This chapter also features various Indian curries, including spicy and fragrant dahl, whose heady blend of ginger, turmeric, mustard seeds, asafoetida, cumin seeds, coriander, and green chillies is classically Indian and extremely inviting. Finally, there is also a dum aloo, which is based on a traditional method of steaming ingredients in their own juices and flavourings. Fragrant with cardamom, cloves, cinnamon, ginger, cumin and chillies, the aromas will be tempting you long before the dish is on the table.

20 mins

Thai yellow vegetable curry

SERVES 6 ✳ **PREPARATION TIME: 20 MINUTES** ✳ **COOKING TIME: 30 MINUTES**

Yellow curries are from Thailand's southern areas and are characterized by their use of spices such as coriander, cumin and turmeric in the paste — the turmeric providing the lovely golden colouring. They are usually of medium strength, wet rather than dry, and delicately spiced.

Yellow curry paste
8 green chillies
5 red Asian shallots, chopped
2 garlic cloves, crushed
1 tablespoon finely chopped coriander (cilantro) stem and root
1 lemon grass stem, white part only, finely chopped
2 tablespoons finely chopped galangal
1 teaspoon ground coriander
1 teaspoon ground cumin
½ teaspoon ground turmeric
½ teaspoon black peppercorns
1 tablespoon lime juice

3 tablespoons oil
1 onion, finely chopped
200 g (7 oz) potatoes, diced
200 g (7 oz) courgette (zucchini), diced
150 g (5½ oz) red pepper (capsicum), diced
100 g (3½ oz) beans, trimmed and halved
50 g (1¾ oz) bamboo shoots, sliced
250 ml (9 fl oz/1 cup) vegetable stock
400 ml (14 fl oz) coconut cream
Thai basil to serve

1. Put all the curry paste ingredients in a food processor, or in a mortar with a pestle, and process or pound to a smooth paste.

2. Heat the oil in a large saucepan, add the onion and cook over medium heat for 4–5 minutes, or until softened and just turning golden. Add 2 tablespoons of the made yellow curry paste and cook, stirring, for 1–2 minutes, or until fragrant.

3. Add all the vegetables and cook, stirring, over high heat for 2 minutes. Pour in the vegetable stock, reduce the heat to medium and cook, covered, for 15–20 minutes, or until the vegetables are tender. Cook, uncovered, over high heat for 5–10 minutes, or until the sauce has reduced slightly.

4. Stir in the coconut cream and season with salt to taste. Bring to the boil, stirring frequently, then reduce the heat and simmer for 5 minutes. Garnish with the Thai basil leaves.

10 mins

Paneer and pea curry

SERVES 5 * **PREPARATION TIME: 10 MINUTES + DRAINING AND WEIGHING DOWN TIME TO MAKE PANEER** * **COOKING TIME: 20 MINUTES**

This substantial yet fragrant dish is an excellent starting point for a vegetarian meal. Paneer is an Indian cottage cheese that is made by heating and curdling milk, then separating the solids. It should always be made freshly, as it lasts only a few days, though it can be bought ready-made.

Paneer
2 litres (70 fl oz/8 cups) milk
80 ml (2½ fl oz/⅓ cup) lemon juice
oil for deep-frying

Curry paste
2 large onions
3 garlic cloves
1 teaspoon grated ginger
1 teaspoon cumin seeds
3 dried red chillies
1 teaspoon cardamom seeds
4 cloves
1 teaspoon fennel seeds
2 pieces cassia bark

500 g (1 lb 2 oz) peas
2 tablespoons oil

Tomato passata
400 ml (14 fl oz) tomato passata
1 tablespoon garam masala
1 teaspoon ground coriander
¼ teaspoon ground turmeric
1 tablespoon cream (whipping)
leaves coriander (cilantro) to serve

1. Put the milk in a large saucepan, bring to the boil, stir in the lemon juice and turn off the heat. Stir the mixture for 1–2 seconds as it curdles. Put in a sieve and leave for 30 minutes for the whey to drain off. Place the paneer curds on a clean, flat surface, cover with a plate, weigh down and leave for at least 4 hours.

2. Put all the curry paste ingredients in a food processor, or in a mortar with a pestle, and process or pound to a smooth paste.

3. Cut the solid paneer into 2 cm (¾ in) cubes. Fill a deep heavy-based saucepan one-third full of oil and heat to 180°C (350°F), or until a cube of bread browns in 15 seconds. Cook the paneer in batches for 2–3 minutes, or until golden. Drain on paper towel. Bring a saucepan of water to the boil, add the peas and cook for 3 minutes, or until tender. Drain and set aside.

4. Heat the oil in a large saucepan, add the curry paste and cook over medium heat for 4 minutes, or until fragrant. Add the puréed tomato, spices, cream and 125 ml (4 fl oz/½ cup) water. Season with salt and simmer over medium heat for 5 minutes. Add the paneer and peas and cook for 3 minutes. Garnish with coriander leaves and serve.

Strain the milk and lemon juice for 30 minutes to help dry out the curds.

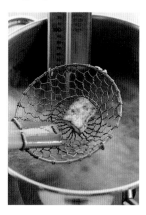

Deep-fry the paneer cubes in batches until golden.

Spinach koftas in yoghurt sauce

SERVES 4 * **PREPARATION TIME: 20 MINUTES** * **COOKING TIME: 30 MINUTES**

Gujarati dishes such as this one are nearly always vegetarian. Curries are typically mild and rely on fresh vegetables, yoghurt, and accompanying pickles and chutneys for extra spice.

Yoghurt sauce

375 g (13 oz/1½ cups) plain yoghurt
35 g (1¼ oz/⅓ cup) besan (chickpea flour)
1 tablespoon oil
2 teaspoons black mustard seeds
1 teaspoon fenugreek seeds
6 curry leaves
1 large onion, finely chopped
3 garlic cloves, crushed
1 teaspoon ground turmeric
½ teaspoon chilli powder

Koftas

450 g (1 lb/1 bunch) spinach, leaves picked off the stems
170 g (6 oz/1½ cups) besan (chickpea flour)
1 red onion, finely chopped
1 ripe tomato, finely diced
2 garlic cloves, crushed
1 teaspoon ground cumin
2 tablespoons chopped coriander (cilantro) leaves

oil for deep-frying
coriander (cilantro) leaves

1. To make the yoghurt sauce whisk the yoghurt, besan and 750 ml (26 fl oz/3 cups) water in a bowl, to a smooth paste. Heat the oil in a heavy-based saucepan or deep frying pan over low heat.

2. Add the mustard and fenugreek seeds and the curry leaves, cover and allow the seeds to pop for 1 minute.

Add the onion and cook for 5 minutes, or until soft and starting to brown.

3. Add the garlic and stir for 1 minute, or until soft. Add the turmeric and chilli powder and stir for 30 seconds. Add the yoghurt mixture, bring to the boil and simmer over low heat for 10 minutes.

4. To make the spinach koftas, blanch the spinach in boiling water for 1 minute and refresh in cold water. Drain, squeeze out any extra water by putting the spinach in a sieve and pressing it against the sides with a spoon. Finely chop the spinach. Combine with the remaining kofta ingredients and up to 3 tablespoons water, a little at a time, adding enough to make the mixture soft but not sloppy. If it becomes too sloppy, add more besan. Shape the mixture into balls by rolling it in dampened hands, using about 1 tablespoon of mixture for each. This should make 12 koftas.

5. Fill a heavy-based saucepan one-third full with oil and heat to 180°C (350°F), or until a cube of bread browns in 15 seconds. Lower the koftas into the oil in batches and fry until golden and crisp. Don't overcrowd the pan. Remove the koftas as they cook, shake off any excess oil and add them to the yoghurt sauce. Gently reheat the yoghurt sauce, garnish with coriander leaves and serve.

Three ways with yoghurt

For diners eating a fiery curry, yoghurt is often a great saviour. It is used in numerous side dishes, specifically designed to accompany spicy meals, and perhaps the most famous examples are Indian raitas. These freshly-made, simple yoghurt preparations can be mixed with grated vegetables, herbs, spices or coconut — whatever suits the curry. Equally creamy and soothing are churris, which also contain buttermilk, and carrot pachadi, a slightly spicier blend.

Churri (yoghurt and buttermilk side dish)

SERVES 4 ✳ PREPARATION TIME: 10 MINUTES ✳ COOKING TIME: 2 MINUTES

Dry-fry 1 teaspoon cumin seeds in a frying pan over medium–high heat for 2–3 minutes, or until fragrant. Allow to cool. Using a mortar with a pestle, or a spice grinder, crush or grind to a powder. Roughly chop a large handful of mint leaves and coriander leaves. Put the mint and coriander in a food processor with a 2 cm (¾ in) piece of ginger and 2 green chillies and process to a smooth paste. Add 310 g (11 oz/1¼ cups) Greek-style yoghurt, 300 ml (10½ fl oz) buttermilk and a pinch of salt to the mixture and process until all the ingredients are well mixed. Season then mix in 1 thinly sliced onion and the ground cumin, reserving a little cumin to sprinkle on top.

Cucumber and tomato raita

SERVES 4 ✳ PREPARATION TIME: 10 MINUTES ✳ COOKING TIME: 2 MINUTES

Put 450 g (1 lb) grated cucumber and 1 large, finely chopped ripe tomato in a sieve for 20 minutes to drain off any excess liquid. Mix them in a bowl with 310 g (11 oz/1¼ cups) Greek-style yoghurt and season to taste with salt. Heat ½ tablespoon of oil in a small saucepan over medium heat, add 1 teaspoon of black mustard seeds then cover and shake the pan until the seeds start to pop. Pour the seeds and oil over the yoghurt. Serve sprinkled with chopped coriander leaves.

Carrot pachadi (yoghurt and carrot side dish)

SERVES 4 ✳ PREPARATION TIME: 10 MINUTES ✳ COOKING TIME: 2 MINUTES

Heat 1 tablespoon oil in a small saucepan over medium heat, add 1 teaspoon black mustard seeds and 2–3 dried chillies then cover and shake the pan until the seeds start to pop. Remove from the heat and immediately stir in a pinch of asafoetida and 1 stalk of curry leaves. Whisk 590 g (1 lb 5 oz/2⅓ cups) Greek-style yoghurt to remove any lumps, then mix in 4 grated carrots. Mix in the mustard seeds, chillies, asafoetida and curry leaves along with the oil, then season with salt, to taste. Garnish with coriander leaves.

10 mins

Sri Lankan aubergine curry

SERVES 6 ✳ **PREPARATION TIME: 10 MINUTES + DRAINING TIME**
COOKING TIME: 15 MINUTES

There are many similarities between Indian and Sri Lankan cooking, but it would be wrong to think they are interchangeable. Crucially, their curry powders differ. Sri Lankan curry powder is made by roasting spices such as cumin, fennel and coriander and has a dark, intense flavour.

1 teaspoon ground turmeric
12 slender aubergines (eggplant),
   cut into 4 cm (1½ in) rounds
oil for deep-frying, plus extra
   2 tablespoons
2 onions, finely chopped
2 tablespoons Sri Lankan
   curry powder
2 garlic cloves, crushed
8 curry leaves, roughly chopped,
   plus extra whole leaves for garnish
½ teaspoon chilli powder
250 ml (9 fl oz/1 cup) coconut cream

Note: Sri Lankan curry powder is available from Asian grocers, and good supermarkets. Regular curry powder can be used in place of Sri Lankan curry powder.

1. Mix half the ground turmeric with 1 teaspoon salt and rub into the aubergine, ensuring the cut surfaces are well coated. Put in a colander and leave for 1 hour. Rinse well and put on crumpled paper towel to remove any excess moisture.

2. Fill a deep heavy-based saucepan one-third full of oil and heat to 180°C (350°F), or until a cube of bread dropped into the oil browns in 15 seconds. Cook the aubergine in batches for 1 minute, or until golden brown. Drain on crumpled paper towel.

3. Heat the extra oil in a large saucepan, add the onion and cook over medium heat for 5 minutes, or until browned. Add the curry powder, garlic, curry leaves, chilli powder, aubergine and remaining turmeric to the pan, and cook for 2 minutes. Stir in the coconut cream and 250 ml (9 fl oz/1 cup) water, and season with salt to taste. Reduce the heat and simmer over low heat for 3 minutes, or until the aubergine is fully cooked and the sauce has thickened slightly. Garnish with extra curry leaves.

Rub the ground turmeric and salt into the aubergines' cut surfaces.

Fry the aubergine in a deep saucepan until golden and tender.

Onion bhaji curry

SERVES 4 * **PREPARATION TIME: 10 MINUTES** * **COOKING TIME: 15 MINUTES**

These bhajis get their distinctive taste and colour from nutty-tasting, yellow besan flour and turmeric. They also contain asafoetida, a dried resin whose pungent aroma has earned it the name 'devil's dung'. It is widely used in India as a flavouring and for its medicinal properties.

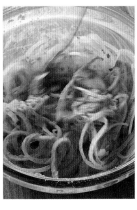

Coat the sliced onion well in the smooth besan batter.

Deep-fry spoonfuls of the bhaji mixture until crisp and golden.

2 tablespoons oil
1 teaspoon grated ginger
2 garlic cloves, crushed
425 g (15 oz) tinned tomatoes, crushed
¼ teaspoon ground turmeric
½ teaspoon chilli powder
1½ teaspoons ground cumin
1 teaspoon ground coriander
1½ tablespoons garam masala
250 ml (9 fl oz/1 cup) cream (whipping)
chopped coriander (cilantro) leaves to serve

Bhajis
125 g (4½ oz/1¼ cups) besan (chickpea flour)
¼ teaspoon ground turmeric
½ teaspoon chilli powder
¼ teaspoon asafoetida
1 onion, thinly sliced
oil for deep-frying

1. Heat the oil in a frying pan, add the ginger and garlic, and cook for 2 minutes, or until fragrant. Add the tomato, turmeric, chilli powder, cumin, coriander and 250 ml (9 fl oz/1 cup) water. Bring to the boil, then reduce the heat and simmer for 5 minutes, or until thickened slightly. Add the garam masala, stir in the cream and simmer for 1–2 minutes. Remove from heat.

2. To make the bhajis, combine the besan, turmeric, chilli powder and asafoetida with 125 ml (4 fl oz/½ cup) water, and salt to taste. Whisk to make a smooth batter, then stir in the onion.

3. Fill a deep heavy-based saucepan one-third full of oil and heat to 160°C (315°F), or until a cube of bread dropped into the oil browns in 30 seconds. Add spoonfuls of the onion mixture in batches and cook for 1–2 minutes, or until golden brown all over, then drain on paper towel. Pour the sauce over the bhajis and garnish with the coriander leaves.

10 mins

Indonesian squash and spinach curry

SERVES 6 * **PREPARATION TIME: 10 MINUTES** * **COOKING TIME: 25 MINUTES**

This curry contains some of the classic ingredients of Indonesian cooking, including candlenuts, shallots, galangal and sambal oelek. Sambal means hot and spicy — which gives you an idea of the dish's taste. This particular sambal is an uncooked mixture of chillies, salt and vinegar or citrus.

Curry paste
3 candlenuts (or macadamia nuts, as an alternative)
1 tablespoon raw peanuts
3 red Asian shallots, chopped
2 garlic cloves
2–3 teaspoons sambal oelek
¼ teaspoon ground turmeric
1 teaspoon grated galangal

2 tablespoons oil
1 onion, finely chopped
600 g (1 lb 5 oz) butternut squash, cut into 2 cm (¾ in) cubes
125 ml (4 fl oz/½ cup) vegetable stock (or as required)
350 g (12 oz) spinach, roughly chopped
400 ml (14 fl oz) coconut cream
¼ teaspoon sugar

1. Put all the curry paste ingredients in a food processor, or in a mortar with a pestle, and process or pound to a smooth paste.

2. Heat the oil in a large saucepan, add the curry paste and cook, stirring, over low heat for 3–5 minutes, or until fragrant. Add the onion and cook for a further 5 minutes, or until softened.

3. Add the squash and half the vegetable stock and cook, covered, for 10 minutes, or until squash is almost cooked through. Add more stock, if required. Add the spinach, coconut cream and sugar, and season with salt. Bring to the boil, stirring constantly, then reduce the heat and simmer for 3–5 minutes, or until the spinach is cooked and the sauce has thickened slightly. Serve immediately.

Process all the paste ingredients to form a smooth paste.

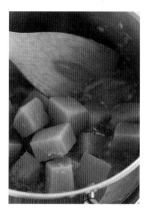

Add the squash with the stock and cook until almost tender.

Hot and sour aubergine curry

SERVES 6 ✳ **PREPARATION TIME: 10 MINUTES + DRAINING TIME**
COOKING TIME: 30 MINUTES

Aubergine goes particularly well with coriander, cumin and coconut — rich, warm flavours — but is surprisingly amenable to a wide range of ingredients, such as the curry-scented fenugreek and anise-flavoured fennel used in this dish.

1 large (about 500 g/1 lb 2 oz)
  aubergine (eggplant)
2 small tomatoes
2 tablespoons oil
3 teaspoons fenugreek seeds
3 teaspoons fennel seeds
4 garlic cloves, crushed
1 large onion, finely diced
4 curry leaves
1½ tablespoons ground coriander
2 teaspoons turmeric
125 ml (4 fl oz/½ cup) tomato juice
2 tablespoons tamarind purée
2 red chillies, finely sliced
125 ml (4 fl oz/½ cup) coconut cream
1 handful leaves coriander
  (cilantro), chopped

Note: Tamarind purée is available from Asian grocers, Thai grocers and supermarkets. Most tamarind products are sold as a concentrate or a pulp with instructions on the label for making the purée by adding water and straining.

1. Cut the aubergine into 2 cm (¾ in) cubes. Sprinkle with ½ teaspoon salt and set aside for 1 hour. Drain and rinse.

2. Chop the tomatoes roughly. Heat the oil in a heavy-based saucepan over medium heat. Add the fenugreek and fennel seeds. When they start to crackle, add the garlic, onion and curry leaves and cook for 3–5 minutes or until onion is transparent. Add the aubergine and stir for 4–5 minutes, or until it begins to soften. Add the ground spices, tomatoes, tomato juice, tamarind and sliced fresh chillies.

3. Bring to the boil, then reduce to a simmer, cover and continue to cook for about 20–25 minutes, or until the aubergine is very soft. Stir in the coconut cream and coriander and season to taste.

Chop the tomatoes roughly, keeping the skin and seeds.

Cook the onion for 3–5 minutes, or until it becomes transparent.

10 mins

Dum aloo

SERVES 6 ✳ **PREPARATION TIME: 10 MINUTES** ✳ **COOKING TIME: 30 MINUTES**

In India, 'dum' means to cook by steaming — it translates as 'to breathe in'. The traditional method was to fill a pot with ingredients, seal the lid with dough and then set the pot over coals. The food would slowly and delicately cook in its own steam and juices.

Curry paste
4 cardamom pods
1 teaspoon grated ginger
2 garlic cloves, crushed
3 red chillies
1 teaspoon cumin seeds
40 g (1½ oz/¼ cup) cashew nuts
1 tablespoon white poppy seeds
1 cinnamon stick
6 cloves

1 kg (2 lb 4 oz) potatoes, cubed
2 onions, roughly chopped
2 tablespoons oil
½ teaspoon ground turmeric
1 teaspoon besan (chickpea flour)
250 g (9 oz/1 cup) plain yoghurt
coriander (cilantro) leaves to garnish

1. Lightly crush the cardamom pods with the flat side of a heavy knife. Remove the seeds, discarding the pods. Put the seeds and the remaining curry paste ingredients in a food processor, or in a mortar with a pestle, and process or pound to a smooth paste.

2. Bring a large saucepan of lightly salted water to the boil. Add the potato and cook for 5–6 minutes, or until just tender, then drain.

3. Put the onions in a food processor and process in short bursts until finely chopped but not puréed. Heat the oil in a large saucepan, add the onion and cook over low heat for 5 minutes. Add the curry paste and cook, stirring, for a further 5 minutes, or until fragrant. Stir in the potato, turmeric, salt to taste and 250 ml (9 fl oz/1 cup) water.

4. Reduce the heat and simmer, tightly covered, for 10 minutes, or until the potato is cooked but not breaking up and the sauce has thickened slightly.

5. Combine the besan with the yoghurt, add to the potato mixture and cook, stirring, over low heat for 5 minutes, or until thickened again. Garnish with the coriander leaves and serve.

Lightly crush the cardamom pods to release the seeds.

Pulse the onions in a food processor until finely chopped.

20 mins

Musaman vegetable curry

SERVES 4–6 * PREPARATION TIME: 20 MINUTES * COOKING TIME: 30 MINUTES

This curry is a good one to try if you are new to curries. It is sumptuously spiced and seasoned without being fiery or overly rich, and has a lightness of flavour not seen in many meat curries. Similarly, the sauce is thick, neither too wet nor dry, and perfect for scooping up with rice or bread.

Musaman curry paste
1 tablespoon oil
1 teaspoon coriander seeds
1 teaspoon cumin seeds
8 cloves
½ teaspoon fennel seeds
4 cardamom seeds
6 red Asian shallots, chopped
3 garlic cloves, chopped
1 teaspoon finely chopped lemon
　grass, white part only
1 teaspoon finely chopped galangal
4 dried long red chillies
1 teaspoon ground nutmeg
1 teaspoon ground white pepper

1 tablespoon oil
250 g (9 oz) baby onions, peeled
500 g (1 lb 2 oz) baby new potatoes
300 g (10½ oz) carrots, cut into
　3 cm (1¼ in) pieces
225 g (8 oz) tinned whole
　baby button mushrooms
　(champignons), drained
1 cinnamon stick
1 kaffir lime (makrut) leaf
1 bay leaf
250 ml (9 fl oz/1 cup) coconut cream
1 tablespoon lime juice
3 teaspoons shaved palm
　sugar (jaggery)
1 tablespoon finely chopped
　Thai basil, plus extra to serve
1 tablespoon crushed roasted
　peanuts

1. Heat the oil in a frying pan over low heat, add the coriander seeds, cumin seeds, cloves, fennel seeds and cardamom seeds, and cook for 1–2 minutes, or until fragrant.

2. Put the spices with the remaining curry paste ingredients in a food processor, or in a mortar with a pestle, and process or pound to a smooth paste. Add a little water if it is too thick.

3. Heat the oil in a large saucepan, add the curry paste and cook, stirring, over medium heat for 2 minutes, or until fragrant. Add the vegetables, cinnamon stick, kaffir lime leaf, bay leaf and enough water to cover (about 500 ml/17 fl oz/2 cups), and bring to the boil. Reduce the heat and simmer, covered, stirring frequently, for 25–30 minutes, or until the vegetables are cooked.

4. Stir in the coconut cream and cook, uncovered, for 3–4 minutes, stirring frequently, until thickened slightly. Stir in the lime juice, palm sugar and chopped basil. Add a little water if the sauce is too dry. Top with the peanuts and basil leaves.

Malaysian hot and sour pineapple curry

SERVES 6 ✳ **PREPARATION TIME: 15 MINUTES** ✳ **COOKING TIME: 20 MINUTES**

Pineapple adds a touch of tart sweetness to curries and is popular in vegetarian meals. Here, it is mixed with hot chillies, creamy coconut and the mellow warmth of cloves and cinnamon to produce a refreshing dish that is a little bit sweet and a little bit spicy.

1 semi-ripe pineapple, cored and cut into chunks
½ teaspoon ground turmeric
1 star anise
1 cinnamon stick, broken into small pieces
7 cloves
7 cardamom pods, bruised
1 tablespoon oil
1 onion, finely chopped
1 teaspoon grated ginger
1 garlic clove, crushed
5 red chillies, chopped
1 tablespoon sugar
3 tablespoons coconut cream

1. Put the pineapple in a saucepan, cover with water and add the turmeric. Put the star anise, cinnamon, cloves and cardamom pods on a square of muslin, and tie securely with string. Add to the pan and cook over medium heat for 10 minutes. Squeeze the bag to extract any flavour, then discard. Reserve the cooking liquid.

2. Heat the oil in a frying pan, add the onion, ginger, garlic and chilli, and cook, stirring, for 1–2 minutes, or until fragrant. Add the pineapple and the cooking liquid, sugar and salt to taste. Cook for 2 minutes, then stir in the coconut cream. Cook, stirring, over low heat for 3–5 minutes, or until the sauce thickens. Serve this curry hot or cold.

pineapple

A native of tropical South America, the pineapple is actually several individual fruit joined together: each of these fruit are the result of numerous unfertilized flowers fused together. To most of us, however, it is a deliciously juicy and sweet fruit, the very emblem of warm weather. Like most fruit, pineapple is best eaten fresh, but it is also used in dishes such as curries, ice creams, sorbets and cakes. Pineapples do not carry on ripening after being picked, so it pays to choose well. Select ones that are heavy for their size and sweetly aromatic.

Three ways with tomatoes

A juicy burst of ripe tomato on the palate can be just the thing when eating a curry. Sweet, cleansing and refreshing, it is an ideal ingredient for a relish. In the first relish here it is combined with lively mint and lime, in the second with fresh coriander and green chillies. Indian pickles are different creatures: designed to stimulate the palate, they are cooked in oil with little or no sugar, and are sharp, spicy and strongly flavoured.

Tomato, lime and mint relish

SERVES 4 * **PREPARATION TIME: 10 MINUTES** * **COOKING TIME: NIL**

Peel 1 lime removing all white pith, finely dice and put into a medium non-metallic bowl with 2 diced tomatoes, 1 finely sliced spring onion (scallion), 2 tablespoons chopped mint, 1 teaspoon fish sauce, 1 teaspoon coconut vinegar (fermented coconut sap, or subsitute with rice vinegar) and 1 teaspoon shaved palm sugar (jaggery). Stir to combine, and allow to sit covered in the refrigerator 30 minutes before serving. This relish goes well with spicy Thai curries.

Tomato and coriander relish

SERVES 4 * **PREPARATION TIME: 10 MINUTES** * **COOKING TIME: NIL**

Mix together 2 diced tomatoes, 3 finely sliced spring onions (scallions), 2 tablespoons finely chopped coriander (cilantro) leaves, 1 finely sliced green chilli, 1 tablespoon lemon juice and 1 teaspoon soft brown sugar. Season with salt and pepper and allow to sit covered in the refrigerator 30 minutes before serving. This relish goes well with Indian and Thai curries.

Indian tomato oil pickle

SERVES 6 * **PREPARATION TIME: 15 MINUTES** * **COOKING TIME: 1 HOUR**

Put 2 teaspoons black or brown mustard seeds and 80 ml (2½ fl oz/⅓ cup) cider vinegar in a small saucepan, and heat over low heat for 12 minutes, or until the seeds just start to pop. The vinegar will be nearly evaporated. Allow to cool. Put the seeds, 1 tablespoon grated ginger and 5 chopped garlic cloves in a food processor, or in a mortar with a pestle, and process or pound to a smooth paste. Heat 3 tablespoons oil in a saucepan, add 3 teaspoons ground cumin and 2 teaspoons ground turmeric and cook, stirring gently, over low heat for 4 minutes, or until fragrant. Add the mustard seed mixture, 1 teaspoon chilli powder, 1 kg (2 lb 4 oz) peeled, seeded and chopped firm, ripe tomatoes, 3 tablespoons sugar and 1 teaspoon salt. Reduce the heat and simmer, stirring occasionally, for 45 minutes, or until thick. Stir through 1 extra tablespoon of cider vinegar. Spoon into clean, warm jars, seal and cool. Refrigerate for up to 1 month. This pickle is best served with Indian curries.

Dhal

SERVES 4–6 ∗ **PREPARATION TIME: 10 MINUTES** ∗ **COOKING TIME: 30 MINUTES**

In India, dhal refers to both the dried pulse and the finished dish. In this recipe, lentils are used, but chickpeas and other beans and peas are also popular. To bolster the simple flavour of the lentils, spices such as cumin and asafoetida are fried in ghee, releasing their earthy aromas.

200 g (7 oz/¾ cup) red lentils
3 thick slices ginger
½ teaspoon ground turmeric
1 tablespoon ghee or oil
2 garlic cloves, crushed
1 onion, finely chopped
½ teaspoon yellow mustard seeds
a pinch asafoetida, optional
1 teaspoon cumin seeds
1 teaspoon ground coriander
2 green chillies, halved lengthways
2 tablespoons lemon juice

1. Put the lentils and 750 ml (26 fl oz/3 cups) water in a saucepan, and bring to the boil. Reduce the heat, add the ginger and turmeric, and simmer, covered, for 20 minutes, or until the lentils are tender. Stir occasionally to prevent the lentils sticking to the pan. Remove the ginger and season the lentil mixture with salt.

2. Heat the ghee or oil in a frying pan, add the garlic, onion and mustard seeds, and cook over medium heat for 5 minutes, or until the onion is golden. Add the asafoetida, cumin seeds, ground coriander and chilli, and cook for 1–2 minutes.

3. Add the onion mixture to the lentils and stir gently to combine. Add 125 ml (4 fl oz/½ cup) water, reduce the heat to low and cook for 4–5 minutes. Stir in the lemon juice and serve.

Cook the onion, mustard seeds and garlic until the onion is golden.

Stir the onion mixture gently through the lentil mixture.

seafood curries

Seafood curries are popular throughout the southern regions of India, and Southeast Asia, where fish and shellfish are readily available. A common ingredient used in Indian fish curries is tamarind, for its cooling, preserving and flavour enhancing qualities. For examples try the goan fish curry, tamarind fish curry or the fish and peanut curry.

When buying fish, it can be tempting to choose safe-looking supermarket-wrapped fillets, but it is far easier to determine whether a fish is fresh by looking at a whole specimen. You can check that the fish smells of the sea — it should not smell 'fishy' — that the flesh is firm, the scales are shiny, and the eyes are clear and bright. Really fresh fish may have gaping mouths and open gill flaps, and some fish, such as salmon and trout, are covered in a clear slime (old slime is opaque). If you require fillets, ask a fishmonger to scale, gut and fillet and, if necessary, skin from a whole fish for you.

It has been said that chillies should be treated with respect, and most of us would agree with that. When scanning the ingredient lists of some of these curries, chillies seem to jump out, regardless of how many other ingredients surround them. Some of us relish the challenge of eating a hot curry; others would prefer to go hungry. But chillies need not — and generally should not — scorch. Rather, they should enhance the overall flavour and fragrance of a dish, with specific chillies being used for their different properties.

Having said that, there are certain curries where no other description besides 'fiery' will do. The jungle curries of Thailand, for example, some of Goa's seafood curries and many Malaysian and Balinese curries fall into this category. Chillies were introduced to Southeast Asia and India in the sixteenth century by traders and spicy dishes can reflect an area's mixed heritage.

If venturing into this taste arena for the first time, just remember that the active agent in chillies, capsaicin, is found mostly in the ribs and seeds of chillies. So, seeding a chilli is a fail-safe way of reducing heat levels. Otherwise, use less than the recipe specifies — you can always add more. As a general guide, the smaller the chilli, the hotter it will be. As well, have plain rice, yoghurt and chilled beer on standby when eating chilli-based dishes.

Balinese seafood curry

SERVES 6 ✳ **PREPARATION TIME: 20 MINUTES + MARINATING TIME**
COOKING TIME: 20 MINUTES

The chilli arrived in Bali fairly recently — with the Portuguese in the sixteenth century — but it has found its way into most dishes. Balinese cuisine is renowned for its spicy and complex flavours, its love of fish and careful preparation of the spice blend.

3 tablespoons lime juice
250 g (9 oz) skinless, firm white fish
　fillets, cut into 3 cm (1¼ in) cubes

Curry paste
1 tablespoon coriander seeds
1 teaspoon shrimp paste
2 tomatoes
5 red chillies
5 garlic cloves, crushed
2 lemon grass stems, white part
　only, chopped
1 tablespoon ground almonds
¼ teaspoon ground nutmeg
1 teaspoon ground turmeric
60 g (2¼ oz/¼ cup) tamarind purée

3 tablespoons oil
2 red onions, chopped
2 red chillies, seeded, sliced
400 g (14 oz) raw prawns (shrimp),
　peeled and deveined, tails intact
250 g (9 oz) squid tubes, cut into
　1 cm (½ in) rings
125 ml (4 fl oz/½ cup) fish stock
Thai basil, shredded, to serve

1. Put the lime juice in a bowl and season with salt and freshly ground black pepper. Add the fish, toss to coat well and leave to marinate for 20 minutes.

2. Dry-fry the coriander seeds and the shrimp paste wrapped in some foil in a frying pan over medium–high heat for 2–3 minutes, or until fragrant. Allow to cool. Using a mortar with a pestle, or a spice grinder, crush or grind the coriander seeds to a powder.

3. Score a cross in the base of the tomatoes, place in a heatproof bowl and cover with boiling water. Leave to stand for 30 seconds, then transfer to cold water and peel the skin away from the cross. Cut the tomatoes in half and scoop out the seeds. Discard the seeds and roughly chop the tomato flesh.

4. Put the crushed coriander seeds, the shrimp paste and tomato with the remaining curry paste ingredients in a food processor, or in a mortar with a pestle, and process or pound to a smooth paste.

5. Heat the oil in a saucepan or wok, add the onion, sliced red chilli and curry paste, and cook, stirring occasionally, over low heat for 10 minutes, or until fragrant. Add the fish and prawns, and stir to coat in the curry paste mixture. Cook for 3 minutes, or until the prawns just turn pink, then add the squid and cook for 1 minute.

6. Add the stock and bring to the boil, then reduce the heat and simmer for 2 minutes, or until the seafood is cooked and tender. Season to taste with salt and freshly ground black pepper. Top with the shredded basil leaves.

Goan fish curry

SERVES 6 ✳ **PREPARATION TIME: 10 MINUTES** ✳ **COOKING TIME: 30 MINUTES**

Goa is situated on India's southwest coast where seafood is a staple ingredient. The other favourite ingredient is coconut, and few dishes are without it. Dishes, including this one, are typically rich, simple and pleasantly spicy with chillies, ginger, turmeric and tamarind.

3 tablespoons oil
1 large onion, finely chopped
4–5 garlic cloves, crushed
2 teaspoons grated ginger
4–6 dried red chillies
1 tablespoon coriander seeds
2 teaspoons cumin seeds
1 teaspoon ground turmeric
¼ teaspoon chilli powder
30 g (1 oz/⅓ cup) desiccated
    coconut
270 ml (9½ fl oz) coconut milk
2 tomatoes, peeled and chopped
2 tablespoons tamarind purée
1 tablespoon white vinegar
6 curry leaves
1 kg (2 lb 4 oz) skinless, firm
    white fish fillets, cut into
    8 cm (3¼ in) pieces

Note: Tamarind purée is available from Asian grocers, Thai grocers and supermarkets. Most tamarind products are sold as a concentrate or a pulp with instructions on the label for making the purée by adding water and straining.

1. Heat the oil in a large saucepan. Add the onion and cook, stirring, over low heat for 6–7 minutes, or until softened and lightly golden. Add the garlic and ginger, and cook for a further 2 minutes.

2. Dry-fry the dried chillies, coriander seeds, cumin seeds, ground turmeric, chilli powder and desiccated coconut in a frying pan over medium–high heat for 2–3 minutes, or until fragrant. Allow to cool. Using a mortar with a pestle, or a spice grinder, crush or grind to a powder.

3. Add the spice mixture, coconut milk, tomato, tamarind, vinegar and curry leaves to the onion mixture. Stir to mix thoroughly, add 250 ml (9 fl oz/1 cup) water and simmer, stirring frequently, for 10 minutes, or until the tomato has softened and the mixture has thickened slightly.

4. Add the fish and cook, covered, over low heat for 10 minutes, or until cooked through. Stir gently once or twice during cooking and add a little water if the mixture is too thick.

Dry-fry the spices and desiccated coconut until aromatic.

Stir the coconut milk into the onion and spice mixture.

Curried squid

SERVES 4 ✳ **PREPARATION TIME: 10 MINUTES** ✳ **COOKING TIME: 15 MINUTES**

This quick and simple curry packs quite a flavour punch. It features the round, earthy flavours of cumin and turmeric, alongside the fresh, sharper flavours of chilli, ginger and lime juice. Versions of this dish are eaten throughout tropical Thailand, Singapore and Malaysia.

1 kg (2 lb 4 oz) squid
1 teaspoon cumin seeds
1 teaspoon coriander seeds
1 teaspoon chilli powder
½ teaspoon ground turmeric
2 tablespoons oil
1 onion, finely chopped
10 curry leaves, plus extra
    for garnish
½ teaspoon fenugreek seeds
4 garlic cloves, crushed
7 cm (2¾ in) piece ginger, grated
100 ml (3½ fl oz) coconut cream
3 tablespoons lime juice

1. Pull the squid heads and tentacles out of their bodies, along with any innards, and discard. Peel off the skins. Rinse the bodies well, pulling out the clear quills, then cut the bodies into 2.5 cm (1 in) rings.

2. Dry-fry the cumin and coriander seeds in a frying pan over medium–high heat for 2–3 minutes, or until fragrant. Allow to cool. Using a mortar with a pestle, or a spice grinder, crush or grind to a powder. Mix the ground cumin and coriander with the chilli powder and ground turmeric. Add the squid and mix well.

3. In a heavy-based frying pan, heat the oil and fry the onion for 5 minutes, or until lightly browned. Add the curry leaves, fenugreek, garlic, ginger and coconut cream. Bring slowly to the boil. Add the squid, then stir well. Simmer for 2–3 minutes, or until cooked and tender. Stir in the lime juice, season and serve garnished with curry leaves.

lime

Wonderfully tangy and aromatic, lime are native to the tropics (possibly originating in Malaysia), where they are widely used in cooking. They are valued as a souring agent and are added to innumerable curries and stews and are particularly good in dipping sauces, chutneys and pickles, some of which can be quite sharp. It is not difficult to make your own lime pickles, but ready-made pickled limes are easily bought from Asian food stores. To get the maximum flavour impact from fresh limes, squeeze them only as needed — for this reason, too, the juice is generally added to a dish only at the end of cooking.

10 mins

Prawns with Thai basil

SERVES 4 * PREPARATION TIME: 10 MINUTES * COOKING TIME: 5 MINUTES

This fragrant and tasty curry couldn't be easier to make. Once the prawns are prepared, the cooking takes only minutes. The sauce should be thick, hot and sweet, so make sure your saucepan or wok is hot enough to reduce the coconut milk as soon as it is added.

Curry paste
2 dried long red chillies
2 lemon grass stems, white part only, finely sliced
2.5 cm (1 in) piece galangal, finely sliced
5 garlic cloves, crushed
4 red Asian shallots, finely chopped
6 coriander (cilantro) roots, finely chopped
1 teaspoon shrimp paste
1 teaspoon ground cumin
3 tablespoons unsalted peanuts, chopped

600 g (1 lb 5 oz) raw prawns (shrimp), peeled and deveined, tails intact
2 tablespoons oil
185 ml (6 fl oz/¾ cup) coconut milk
2 teaspoons fish sauce
2 teaspoons shaved palm sugar (jaggery)
1 handful Thai basil leaves to serve

1. Soak the chillies in boiling water for 5 minutes, or until soft. Remove the seeds and stems and chop. Put the chillies and the remaining curry paste ingredients in a food processor, or in a mortar with a pestle, and process or pound to a smooth paste.

2. Cut each prawn along the back so it opens like a butterfly (leave each prawn joined along the base and at the tail). Heat the oil in a saucepan or wok and stir-fry 2 tablespoons of the curry paste over a medium heat for 2 minutes, or until fragrant.

3. Add the coconut milk, fish sauce and palm sugar and cook for a few seconds. Add the prawns and cook for 3–4 minutes or until cooked through. Taste, then adjust the seasoning if necessary. Serve garnished with Thai basil.

basil

There are three main types of basil used in Thai cuisine. The most important by far is Thai basil, also known as Thai sweet basil. This variety has purplish stems, lush, deep green leaves and an aniseed aroma and flavour. It is added liberally to a wide range of dishes. Next up is holy basil, which is available in two types: red- and white-stemmed. Highly perfumed and with a peppery taste, holy basil is always cooked to release its flavour. The final type is lemon basil, also called mint basil. As its name suggests, it has a fresh, tangy scent and flavour and is delicious with fish, poultry and sweet drinks and desserts.

Three ways with coconut

The coconut palm grows all over Asia and such is the importance of the fruit that it is known as shrifal, or 'fruit of lustre', in parts of India. Countless curries are based on coconut milk or cream, which are also used in soups, salads and pastries. The desiccated flesh is used in garnishes, chutneys, raitas and desserts. When served alongside or after a spicy curry, coconut sides and drinks can either soothe and refresh palates, or add a little extra spiciness to the main event.

Coconut and coriander chutney
SERVES 4 ＊ **PREPARATION TIME: 10 MINUTES** ＊ **COOKING TIME: NIL**

Put 90 g (3¼ oz) roughly chopped coriander (cilantro), including the roots, 25 g (1 oz/¼ cup) desiccated coconut, 1 tablespoon soft brown sugar, 1 tablespoon grated ginger, 1 chopped small onion, 2 tablespoons lemon juice, 1–2 seeded green chillies and 1 teaspoon salt in a food processor and process for 1 minute, or until finely chopped. Refrigerate until ready to serve. There are numerous variations, depending on region and tastes. Try substituting 1 handful of roughly chopped mint leaves for the coriander in this recipe, or add 5 roughly chopped spring onions (scallions), including the green part, instead of the onion. If you prefer more fire in your chutney, do not remove the seeds from the chillies.

Coconut and pineapple cooler
SERVES 4 ＊ **PREPARATION TIME: 10 MINUTES + FREEZING TIME** ＊ **COOKING TIME: NIL**

Peel and chop 2 pineapples and juice through a juice extractor. Transfer the pineapple juice to a large jug and stir through 500 ml (17 fl oz/2 cups) of coconut milk. Pour 250 ml (9 fl oz/1 cup) of the mixture into 16 holes of an ice-cube tray and freeze. Chill the remaining mixture. When the ice cubes have frozen, pour the juice mixture into 4 glasses, add the ice cubes and garnish with mint and pineapple leaves.

Fresh coconut chutney
SERVES 4 ＊ **PREPARATION TIME: 10 MINUTES** ＊ **COOKING TIME: 3 MINUTES**

Soak 1 teaspoon chana dhal (gram lentils) and 1 teaspoon urad dhal (black lentils) in cold water for 2 hours, then drain well. Put the grated flesh from half a fresh coconut, 2 seeded and chopped green chillies and ½ teaspoon salt in a food processor, or in a mortar with a pestle, and process or pound to a smooth paste. Heat 1 tablespoon oil in a small saucepan and add 1 teaspoon black mustard seeds and the dhals, then cover and shake the pan until they pop. Add 5 curry leaves and fry for 1 minute, or until the dhal browns. Add these ingredients to the coconut with 1 teaspoon tamarind purée and mix well.

10 mins

Fish in yoghurt curry

SERVES 4 ∗ PREPARATION TIME: 10 MINUTES ∗ COOKING TIME: 30 MINUTES

The creamy texture of this dish belies the depth of flavour it has from the cumin, coriander and turmeric. Thick yoghurt is an excellent way to protect the fish during cooking and also absorbs some of the sting from the chillies. For best results use a thick, set yoghurt.

1 kg (2 lb 4 oz) skinless, firm white fish fillets
3 tablespoons oil
1 onion, chopped
2 tablespoons finely chopped ginger
6 garlic cloves, crushed
1 teaspoon ground cumin
2 teaspoons ground coriander
¼ teaspoon ground turmeric
1 teaspoon garam masala
185 g (6½ oz/¾ cup) Greek-style yoghurt
4 long green chillies, seeded, finely chopped
coriander (cilantro) leaves to serve

1. Cut each fish fillet into four pieces and thoroughly pat them dry. Heat the oil in a heavy-based frying pan over medium heat and fry the onion for 5 minutes, or until softened and lightly browned. Add the ginger, garlic and spices and stir for 2 minutes. Add the yoghurt and green chilli and bring to the boil, then cover and simmer for 10 minutes.

2. Slide in the pieces of fish and continue to simmer for 10–12 minutes, or until the fish flakes easily and is cooked through. Don't overcook or the fish will give off liquid and the sauce will split.

3. Garnish with coriander leaves and serve immediately. If you let the dish sit, the fish may give off liquid and make the sauce more runny.

ginger

Knobbly ginger 'hands' are familiar to most cooks today, but it can still be surprising to discover that the plant has been cultivated for millennia in China. Thought to be indigenous to northern India, ginger is used extensively in Chinese, Indian and Asian cooking for its sweet aroma and peppery, tangy flavour. It is featured in soups, curries and salads, and in relishes for its clean, digestive qualities. When buying, look for plump examples with pink-beige skin. The flesh inside should be moist and creamy-lemon. Ginger is also available dried, ground and pickled.

15 mins

Spicy prawns

SERVES 4–6 * **PREPARATION TIME: 15 MINUTES** * **COOKING TIME: 30 MINUTES**

Turmeric is at the heart of so many curries. It imparts not just colour, but also a subtle aroma and earthy, slightly bitter flavour. Using ground turmeric is easy and convenient but buy some fresh turmeric root if you see it. It looks similar to old ginger, but inside it is wonderfully golden.

1 kg (2 lb 4 oz) raw prawns
   (shrimp), peeled and deveined,
   tails intact (reserve shells
   and heads)
1 teaspoon ground turmeric
3 tablespoons oil
2 onions, finely chopped
4–6 garlic cloves, crushed
1–2 green chillies, seeded
   and chopped
2 teaspoons ground cumin
2 teaspoons ground coriander
1 teaspoon paprika
90 g (3¼ oz/⅓ cup) plain yoghurt
80 ml (2½ fl oz/⅓ cup) thickened
   (whipping) cream
1 large handful coriander
   (cilantro) leaves, chopped

1. Bring 1 litre (35 fl oz/4 cups) water to the boil in a saucepan. Add the reserved prawn shells and heads, reduce the heat and simmer for 2 minutes. Skim any scum that forms on the surface during cooking. Strain, discard the shells and heads and return the liquid to the pan. You will need about 750 ml (26 fl oz/3 cups) liquid (make up with water if necessary). Add the turmeric and peeled prawns, and cook for 1 minute, or until the prawns just turn pink, then remove the prawns. Increase the heat to high and reduce stock by a third. Reserve the stock.

2. Meanwhile heat the oil in a large saucepan. Add the onion and cook over a medium heat, stirring, for 5 minutes, or until lightly golden brown. Add the garlic and chilli, and cook for 1–2 minutes, then add the cumin, coriander and paprika, and cook, stirring, for 1–2 minutes, or until fragrant.

3. Gradually add the reserved stock, bring to the boil and cook, stirring occasionally, for 15–20 minutes, or until the mixture has reduced by a third and thickened. Remove from the heat and stir in the yoghurt. Add the prawns and stir over low heat for 2–3 minutes, or until the prawns are warmed through. Do not boil. Stir in the cream and coriander leaves. Cover and leave to stand for 15 minutes to allow the flavours to infuse. Reheat gently and serve.

Simmer the prawn shells and heads, skimming the surface.

Poach the prawns in the stock until just pink and curled.

Tamarind fish curry

SERVES 4 * PREPARATION TIME: 15 MINUTES + MARINATING TIME
COOKING TIME: 30 MINUTES

Tamarind is widely used in Indian and Southeast Asian cooking for its sweet–sour flavour and souring properties. Here, the tamarind is balanced by full-bodied peppercorns, cumin and coriander; made aromatic with pungent saffron and sweet cardamom; and creamy with thick yoghurt.

600 g (1 lb 5 oz) skinless, firm
   white fish fillets
1 teaspoon turmeric
a pinch powdered saffron
3 garlic cloves, crushed
2 teaspoons lemon juice
1 teaspoon cumin seeds
2 tablespoons coriander seeds
1 teaspoon white peppercorns
4 cardamom pods, bruised
2½ tablespoons finely chopped
   ginger
2 red chillies, finely sliced
2 tablespoons oil
1 onion, chopped
1 red pepper (capsicum), cut into
   2 cm (¾ in) squares
1 green pepper (capsicum), cut into
   2 cm (¾ in) squares
4 plum (Roma) tomatoes, diced
2 tablespoons tamarind purée
185 g (6½ oz/¾ cup) plain yoghurt
2 tablespoons chopped coriander
   (cilantro) leaves

1. Rinse the fish fillets and pat dry. Prick the fillets with a fork. Combine the turmeric, saffron, garlic, lemon juice and 1 teaspoon of salt then rub over the fish fillets. Refrigerate for 2–3 hours.

2. Dry-fry the cumin seeds, coriander seeds, peppercorns and cardamom in a frying pan over medium–high heat for 2–3 minutes, or until fragrant. Allow to cool. Using a mortar with a pestle, or a spice grinder, crush or grind to a powder and combine with the ginger and chillies.

3. Heat the oil in a heavy-based saucepan over medium heat and add the chopped onion, red and green peppers, and ground spice mix. Cook gently for 5–10 minutes, or until aromatic and the onion is transparent. Increase heat to high, add the diced tomatoes, 250 ml (9 fl oz/1 cup) of water and the tamarind purée. Bring to the boil then reduce to a simmer and cook for 15–20 minutes.

4. Rinse the paste off the fish and chop into 3 cm (1¼ in) pieces. Add to the pan and continue to simmer for 10 minutes. Stir in the yoghurt and chopped coriander and serve.

Rub the saffron mixture into the fish fillets and leave for 2–3 hours.

Dry-fry the spices until aromatic then grind to a fine powder.

Jungle curry prawns

SERVES 6 ✳ **PREPARATION TIME: 15 MINUTES** ✳ **COOKING TIME: 15 MINUTES**

Be warned: jungle curries are generally hot curries! Traditionally, there is no coconut to absorb the heat of the chillies. However, they usually also feature plenty of fresh spices and vegetables, as is the case here. The final flavour is aromatic, hot and salty, but not scorching.

Jungle curry paste
10–12 dried red chillies
1 teaspoon white pepper
4 red Asian shallots
4 garlic cloves
1 lemon grass stem, white part
  only, chopped
1 tablespoon finely chopped
  galangal
2 coriander (cilantro) roots
1 tablespoon finely chopped ginger
1 tablespoon dry roasted
  shrimp paste

1 tablespoon peanut oil
1 garlic clove, crushed
1 tablespoon fish sauce
30 g (1 oz/¼ cup) ground
  candlenuts (or macadamia nuts,
  as an alternative)
300 ml (10½ fl oz) fish stock
1 tablespoon whisky
3 kaffir lime (makrut) leaves, torn
600 g (1 lb 5 oz) raw prawns
  (shrimp) peeled, and deveined,
  tails intact
1 small carrot, quartered
  lengthways, sliced thinly on
  the diagonal
150 g (5½ oz) yard-long (snake)
  beans, cut into 2 cm (¾ in)
  lengths
50 g (1¾ oz/¼ cup) bamboo shoots
Thai basil to serve

1. Soak the chillies in boiling water for 5 minutes, or until soft. Remove the stem and seeds, then chop. Put the chillies and the remaining curry paste ingredients in a food processor, or in a mortar with a pestle, and process or pound to a smooth paste. Add a little water if it is too thick.

2. Heat a wok over medium heat, add the oil and swirl to coat. Add the garlic and 3 tablespoons of the curry paste and cook, stirring, for 5 minutes. Add the fish sauce, ground candlenuts, fish stock, whisky, kaffir lime leaves, prawns, carrot, beans and bamboo shoots. Bring to the boil, then reduce the heat and simmer for 5 minutes, or until the prawns and vegetables are cooked. Top with Thai basil and serve.

15 mins

Snapper with green bananas and mango

SERVES 4 * **PREPARATION TIME: 15 MINUTES** * **COOKING TIME: 20 MINUTES**

This impressive-looking curry is richly flavoured with spices, herbs and tropical fruit. Robust fruit like green banana makes an interesting textural addition to curries — the banana is very starchy, more like a vegetable than a fruit, and will help to thicken the curry.

Curry paste
3 teaspoons coriander seeds
1 teaspoon cumin seeds
2–3 dried long red chillies
2 lemon grass stems, white part only, finely sliced
3 red Asian shallots, finely chopped
2 garlic cloves, crushed
1 teaspoon ground turmeric
1 teaspoon shrimp paste

1 teaspoon ground turmeric
1 small green banana or plantain, thinly sliced
3 tablespoons coconut cream
1 tablespoon fish sauce
1 teaspoon shaved palm sugar (jaggery)
400 g (14 oz) snapper or other skinless, firm white fish fillets, cut into large cubes
315 ml (10¾ fl oz/1¼ cups) coconut milk
1 small, just ripe mango, cut into thin slices
1 long green chilli, finely sliced
12 Thai basil leaves

1. Dry-fry the coriander and cumin seeds in a frying pan over medium–high heat for 2–3 minutes, or until fragrant. Allow to cool. Using a mortar with a pestle, or a spice grinder, crush or grind to a powder.

2. Soak the chillies in boiling water for 5 minutes, or until soft. Remove the stem and seeds, then chop. Put the chillies, the ground coriander and cumin seeds with the remaining curry paste ingredients in a food processor, or in a mortar with a pestle, and process or pound to a smooth paste. Add a little oil if it is too thick.

3. Bring a small saucepan of water to the boil. Add 1 teaspoon salt, turmeric and banana slices and simmer for 10 minutes, then drain.

4. Put the coconut cream in a saucepan, bring to a rapid simmer over medium heat, stirring occasionally, and cook for 5–10 minutes, or until the mixture 'splits' (the oil starts to separate). Add 2 tablespoons of the made curry paste, stir well to combine and cook until fragrant. Add the fish sauce and sugar and cook for another 2 minutes or until the mixture begins to darken.

5. Add the fish pieces and stir well to coat the fish in the curry mixture. Slowly add the coconut milk until it has all been incorporated.

6. Add the banana, mango, green chilli and the basil leaves to the pan and gently stir to combine all the ingredients. Cook for a further 1–2 minutes, then serve.

20 mins

Scallops and prawns chu chee

SERVES 4 ✳ PREPARATION TIME: 20 MINUTES ✳ COOKING TIME: 25 MINUTES

Chu chee curry paste is the traditional Thai flavour base for seafood. It is similar to a red curry paste, in that dried red chillies dominate, but the proportion of aromatics such as galangal, lemon grass, kaffir lime (makrut) leaves and coriander (cilantro) are greater.

Chu chee curry paste
10 dried long red chillies
1 teaspoon coriander seeds
1 tablespoon shrimp paste
1 tablespoon white peppercorns
10 kaffir lime (makrut) leaves, finely shredded
10 red Asian shallots, chopped
2 teaspoons finely grated kaffir lime (makrut) zest
1 tablespoon chopped coriander (cilantro) stem and root
1 lemon grass stem, white part only, finely chopped
3 tablespoons chopped galangal
1 tablespoon chopped krachai, optional (see note)
6 garlic cloves, crushed

540 ml (18½ fl oz) coconut cream (do not shake the tins)
500 g (1 lb 2 oz) scallops, with roe removed
500 g (1 lb 2 oz) raw king prawns (shrimp), peeled and deveined, tails intact
2–3 tablespoons fish sauce
2–3 tablespoons palm sugar (jaggery)
8 kaffir lime (makrut) leaves, finely shredded
2 red chillies, thinly sliced
1 large handful Thai basil

Note: Krachai (bottled lesser galangal) is available from Asian food stores. It can be omitted from the paste if unavailable.

1. Soak the chillies in boiling water for 5 minutes, or until soft. Remove the stem and seeds, then chop. Dry-fry the coriander seeds, shrimp paste wrapped in foil, and peppercorns in a frying pan over medium–high heat for 2–3 minutes, or until fragrant. Allow to cool. Using a mortar with a pestle, or a spice grinder, crush or grind the coriander and peppercorns to a powder.

2. Put the chopped chillies, shrimp paste and ground coriander and peppercorns with the remaining curry paste ingredients in a food processor, or in a mortar with a pestle, and process or pound to a smooth paste.

3. Put the thick coconut cream from the top of the tins in a saucepan, bring to a rapid simmer over medium heat, stirring occasionally, and cook for 5–10 minutes, or until the mixture 'splits' (the oil starts to separate). Stir in 3 tablespoons of the curry paste, reduce the heat and simmer for 10 minutes, or until fragrant.

4. Stir in the remaining coconut cream, scallops and prawns, and cook for 5 minutes, or until tender. Add the fish sauce, palm sugar, kaffir lime leaves and chilli, and cook for 1 minute. Stir in half the Thai basil and garnish with the remaining leaves.

Fish and peanut curry

SERVES 6 ✳ **PREPARATION TIME: 15 MINUTES** ✳ **COOKING TIME: 25 MINUTES**

One of the star ingredients in this dish is crisp fried onion, which can be bought from Asian food stores, or easily prepared at home (see note below). Dried spices and sour tamarind are also used to nicely balance the creamy, nutty flavours of this dish.

50 g (1¾ oz/⅓ cup) sesame seeds
½ teaspoon cayenne pepper
¼ teaspoon ground turmeric
1 tablespoon desiccated coconut
2 teaspoons ground coriander
½ teaspoon ground cumin
40 g (1½ oz/½ cup) crisp fried onion (see note)
5 cm (2 in) piece ginger, chopped
2 garlic cloves, chopped
3 tablespoons tamarind purée
1 tablespoon crunchy peanut butter
1 tablespoon roasted peanuts
8 curry leaves, plus extra, to serve
1 kg (2 lb 4 oz) skinless, firm white fish fillets, cut into 2 cm (¾ in) cubes
1 tablespoon lemon juice

Note: To make crisp fried onion at home, very thinly slice 1 onion, then dry on paper towel for 10 minutes. Fill a deep, heavy-based saucepan one-third full of oil and heat to 160°C (315°F), or until a cube of bread dropped into the oil browns in 30 seconds. Fry the onions for up to 1 minute, or until crisp and golden. Drain well, cool and store in an airtight container for up to 2 weeks. Use as a garnish and flavour enhancer for curries, rice and noodle dishes.

1. Put the sesame seeds in a heavy-based frying pan, over medium heat, and stir 2–3 minutes, or until golden. Add the cayenne pepper, turmeric, coconut, ground coriander and ground cumin and stir for a further minute, or until aromatic. Set aside to cool.

2. Put the fried onions, ginger, garlic, tamarind, 1 teaspoon salt, peanut butter, roasted peanuts, sesame spice mix and 500 ml (17 fl oz/2 cups) hot water in a food processor and process until mixture reaches a smooth, thick consistency.

3. Put the sauce and curry leaves into a heavy-based frying pan over medium heat and bring to a simmer. Cover and simmer over low heat for 15 minutes, then add the fish in a single layer. Simmer, covered, for a further 5 minutes, or until the fish is just cooked through. Gently stir through the lemon juice, and season well to taste. Garnish with curry leaves and serve.

Stir the sesame seeds over medium heat until lightly golden.

Add the fish in a single layer to the simmering sauce.

The perfect curry paste

Commercially produced curry pastes certainly have their place, but nothing will ever compete with a fresh, home-made batch — the benefits far outweighing the effort. Not only will your curry have better flavour but there is a certain amount of joy involved in selecting, sniffing and touching fresh, exotic ingredients then taking the time and care to finely grind them, releasing fresh and spicy aromas into your home. It is the aromas and flavours generated by the release of natural oils during the grinding process that makes a made-from-scratch curry unique and irresistible. You can also keep excess curry paste in an airtight container in the refrigerator for one week, or in the freezer for up to two months.

If you follow the guidelines below in conjunction with individual curry recipes you will achieve great results every time. Firstly, any fresh produce required should be just that — fresh, as well as firm, crisp, unblemished and aromatic. Shrivelled up leafy herbs and chillies, dried up garlic, ginger and lemon grass or soft onions will result in an inferior product. To obtain the maximum flavour and aroma from your curry pastes, put fresh ingredients into the hollow of a mortar then pound and grind with a pestle until the mixture becomes pulpy then as smooth as possible. This can take some time but it is worth it, not only flavourwise but for ensuring your curry has a consistent texture.

Spices should be bought in small quantities and used up quickly as they deteriorate when exposed to air. Fresh whole spices contain more essential oils — and therefore flavour — than pre-ground or those that have been sitting in the cupboard for some time. Dry fry the spices in a frying pan over medium–high heat for 2–3 minutes, or until fragrant, to release the oils and make the spices more brittle for grinding. To grind the spices, allow them to cool then tip into a mortar and pound with a pestle until finely ground. The grinding releases the flavours and aromas and allows them to travel more evenly through the curry.

Creamy prawn curry

SERVES 4 ✴ **PREPARATION TIME: 15 MINUTES** ✴ **COOKING TIME: 15 MINUTES**

Creamy, yes, but also fragrant with cloves, cardamom, cinnamon and Indian bay leaves. If possible use Indian bay leaves and not the European variety. They should more accurately be called cassia leaves, as they are from the cassia tree. They are spicy and refreshing, with a sweet, woody aroma.

500 g (1 lb 2 oz) tiger prawns
   (shrimp), peeled and deveined,
   with tails intact
1½ tablespoons lemon juice
3 tablespoons oil
½ onion, finely chopped
½ teaspoon ground turmeric
1 cinnamon stick
4 cloves
7 cardamom pods, bruised
5 Indian bay (cassia) leaves
2 cm (¾ in) piece ginger, grated
3 garlic cloves, crushed
1 teaspoon chilli powder
170 ml (5½ fl oz/⅔ cup)
   coconut milk

Note: Indian bay leaves can be found in Asian Grocers. If necessary, 1 bay leaf can be used in place of every 2 Indian bay leaves.

1. Put the prawns in a bowl, add the lemon juice, then toss together and leave them for 5 minutes. Rinse the prawns under running cold water and pat dry with paper towel.

2. Heat the oil in a heavy-based frying pan over medium heat and fry the onion for 5 minutes, or until lightly browned. Add the turmeric, cinnamon, cloves, cardamom, bay leaves, ginger and garlic, and fry for 1 minute. Add the chilli powder, coconut milk, and salt to taste, and slowly bring to the boil. Reduce the heat and simmer for 2 minutes.

3. Add the prawns, return to the boil, then reduce the heat and simmer for 5 minutes, or until the prawns are cooked through and the sauce is thick.

Add the spices to the browned onion and cook until fragrant.

Simmer the prawns gently until just curled and cooked through.

20 mins

Fish koftas in tomato curry sauce

SERVES 6 * **PREPARATION TIME: 20 MINUTES** * **COOKING TIME: 30 MINUTES**

Koftas were originally invented by the arabs and have proved to be immensely versatile. In this dish, both the kofta and the sauce are quite aromatic; however, the spices complement each other rather than compete. The sauce is slightly sweet and earthy, while the kofta are rich and spicy.

Koftas
750 g (1 lb 10 oz) skinless, firm
   white fish fillets, roughly
   chopped
1 onion, chopped
2–3 garlic cloves, crushed
1 tablespoon grated ginger
4 tablespoons chopped coriander
   (cilantro) leaves
1 teaspoon garam masala
¼ teaspoon chilli powder
1 egg, lightly beaten
oil for shallow-frying

Tomato curry sauce
2 tablespoons oil
1 large onion, finely chopped
3–4 garlic cloves, crushed
1 tablespoon grated ginger
1 teaspoon ground turmeric
1 teaspoon ground cumin
1 teaspoon ground coriander
1 teaspoon garam masala
¼ teaspoon chilli powder
800 g (1 lb 12 oz) tinned
   tomatoes, crushed
3 tablespoons chopped coriander
   (cilantro) leaves, plus extra
   sprigs, to serve

1. Put the fish in a food processor, or in a mortar with a pestle, and process or pound to a smooth paste. Add the onion, garlic, ginger, coriander leaves, garam masala, chilli powder and egg, and process or pound until well combined. Using wetted hands, form 1 tablespoon of the mixture into a ball. Repeat with the remaining mixture.

2. To make the tomato curry sauce, heat the oil in a large saucepan, add the onion, garlic and ginger, and cook, stirring frequently, over medium heat for 8 minutes, or until lightly golden.

3. Add the spices and cook, stirring, for 2 minutes, or until aromatic. Add the tomato and 250 ml (9 fl oz/1 cup) water, then reduce the heat and simmer, stirring frequently, for 15 minutes, or until reduced and thickened.

4. Meanwhile, heat the oil in a large frying pan to the depth of 2 cm (¾ in). Add the fish koftas in 3 or 4 batches and cook for 3 minutes, or until browned all over. Drain on paper towel.

5. Add the koftas to the sauce and simmer over low heat for 5 minutes, or until heated through. Gently fold in the coriander, season with salt and serve garnished with coriander sprigs.

15 mins

Thai hot and sour prawn and squash curry

SERVES 4 ✳ **PREPARATION TIME: 15 MINUTES** ✳ **COOKING TIME: 25 MINUTES**

Flavoured with red curry paste, perfumed by kaffir lime (makrut) leaves, and seasoned with tamarind, fish sauce, lime juice and chillies, this delicious curry is a real meal-in-a-bowl. The flavours are well-balanced, with a bit of bite and a lovely tangy taste, but do not overpower the prawns (shrimp).

250 g (9 oz) butternut squash
1 Lebanese (short) cucumber
400 ml (14 fl oz/1⅔ cups) coconut cream (do not shake the tin)
1½ tablespoons ready-made red curry paste
3 tablespoons fish sauce
2 tablespoons shaved palm sugar (jaggery)
400 g (14 oz) tinned straw mushrooms, drained
500 g (1 lb 2 oz) raw prawns (shrimp), peeled and deveined, tails intact
2 tablespoons tamarind purée
2 red chillies, chopped
1 tablespoon lime juice
4 kaffir lime (makrut) leaves
4 coriander (cilantro) roots, chopped
1 small handful bean sprouts, to serve
1 small handful coriander (cilantro) leaves to serve

1. Peel the squash and chop into 2 cm (¾ in) cubes. Peel and cut the cucumber in half lengthways, then scrape out the seeds with a teaspoon and thinly slice.

2. Put the thick coconut cream from the top of the tin in a saucepan, bring to a rapid simmer over medium heat, stirring occasionally, and cook for 5–10 minutes, or until the mixture 'splits' (the oil starts to separate). Add the paste and stir for 2–3 minutes, or until fragrant. Add the fish sauce and palm sugar and stir until dissolved.

3. Add the remaining coconut cream, squash, and 3 tablespoons of water, cover and bring to boil. Reduce to a simmer and cook for 10 minutes, or until squash is just starting to become tender. Add the straw mushrooms, prawns, cucumber, tamarind, chilli, lime juice, kaffir lime leaves and coriander roots. Cover, increase the heat and bring to the boil again before reducing to a simmer and cooking for 3–5 minutes, or until the prawns are just cooked through. Garnish with bean sprouts and coriander leaves.

chillies

It's hard to believe chillies aren't indigenous to Asia, such is their importance in cuisines stretching from India to Indonesia. However, since their introduction to the region in the sixteenth century, they have become inextricably linked with the local diets. There are thousands of varieties of chilli plants, with pods in an assortment of shapes, sizes and colours, and varying in their degree of hotness from gentle to positively painful. But chillies are not merely hot; each has its own flavour, and dried and fresh chillies also taste very different. Some popular varieties used in curries include cayenne, kashmiri and bird's eye chillies.

meat curries

Meat curries are traditionally renowned for their long slow cooking, which is how their intense rich flavours develop. Many of the regions recognised for their curries are poor and therefore rely on the cheaper cuts of meat, that require longer slower cooking. Over half the recipes that feature in this section are cooked within 30 minutes, but to give meat curries the justice they deserve, some of the traditional slower cooked recipes have been included, all of which can be prepared in under 30 minutes, and then left to cook slowly.

The pleasure of many curries begins with the aroma that is released at the start of cooking, as dried spices roast and crackle in the wok or pan. Spices such as cumin, fennel, coriander seeds, turmeric and curry leaves all bring a warm, rounded, toasty aroma and flavour to curries. For these curries, aroma is of equal importance to flavour and texture.

Taking the time to grind and roast your own spices may seem like a luxury these days but it is one of the best, and most enjoyable, ways to learn about the different qualities of the spices that go into a curry. Coriander seeds, for example, have a sweet, heady aroma, suggestive of pine and pepper, while warm and bitter cumin is immediately distinctive. Fennel seeds have a subtle anise aroma and warm, sweet, intense flavour that mellows on roasting. Different again are potent cloves, with their sharp and woody flavours contributing to many curry powders, and versatile, pungent turmeric. Hidden within the unassuming dull brown skin of this root is a vibrantly coloured golden interior that, as a ground powder, is used in countless curries to balance and enhance the other flavours.

Many of these spices have been known for millennia — coriander is mentioned in ancient Sanskrit texts, and turmeric was included in an Assyrian manuscript dating back to 600 bc. The longevity of these spices is reflected in some of the recipes in this chapter. Both aromatic and slow-cooking rogan josh and the equally luxurious lamb dhansak from India have their origins in Persia, whose traditional cooking is renowned for its subtle and sophisticated use of spices. A classic of one-pot cooking, the meat is tender and the flavour welcoming. There is also a dish from Sri Lanka, whose curry powders typically feature cardamom, cloves, cumin seeds, coriander and cinnamon, and are characterized by a dark, roasted flavour and aroma. Overall, the curries in this chapter share a depth of sensuous flavour and aroma that is not always anticipated — which makes cooking and eating them all the more enjoyable.

15 mins

Butter chicken

SERVES 4–6 ✳ **PREPARATION TIME: 15 MINUTES** ✳ **COOKING TIME: 30 MINUTES**

For many westerners, this famous dish is their first experience of Indian food. Based on tandoori chicken, but without the tandoor, it is a rich blend of aromatic spices, butter or ghee, yoghurt and tomato purée. When done properly, it is sumptuous and velvety, not merely creamy.

2 tablespoons peanut oil

1 kg (2 lb 4 oz) chicken thigh fillets, quartered

100 g (3½ oz) butter or ghee

3 teaspoons garam masala

2 teaspoons sweet paprika

1 tablespoon ground coriander

1 tablespoon finely chopped ginger

3 teaspoons ground cumin

2 garlic cloves, crushed

¼ teaspoon chilli powder

1 cinnamon stick

5 cardamom pods, bruised

2½ tablespoons tomato purée (paste)

1 tablespoon sugar

90 g (3¼ oz/⅓ cup) plain yoghurt

185 ml (6 fl oz/¾ cup) cream (whipping)

1 tablespoon lemon juice

1. Heat a frying pan or wok until very hot, add 1 tablespoon oil and swirl to coat. Add half the chicken thigh fillets and stir-fry for 4 minutes, or until browned. Remove from the pan. Add extra oil, as needed, and cook the remaining chicken, then remove.

2. Reduce the heat, add the butter to the pan or wok and melt. Add the garam masala, sweet paprika, coriander, ginger, cumin, garlic, chilli powder, cinnamon stick and cardamom pods, and stir-fry for 1 minute, or until fragrant. Return the chicken to the pan and mix in the spices so it is well coated.

3. Add the tomato purée and sugar, and simmer, stirring, for 15 minutes, or until the chicken is tender and the sauce has thickened. Add the yoghurt, cream and lemon juice and simmer for 5 minutes, or until the sauce has thickened slightly.

Stir-fry the spices in a frying pan or wok until fragrant.

Stir in the tomato purée and sugar and simmer.

Five-spice pork curry

SERVES 4 ∗ **PREPARATION TIME: 15 MINUTES** ∗ **COOKING TIME: 25 MINUTES**

This dish draws on various influences to create a spicy, salty and fragrant dish. Five-spice is widely used in many Asian countries besides China, and here it is mixed with kecap manis, a thick, sweet dark soy sauce from Indonesia. Five-spice is strongly flavoured, so use sparingly.

500 g (1 lb 2 oz) pork spare ribs
1½ tablespoons oil
2 garlic cloves, crushed
190 g (6¾ oz) fried tofu puffs
1 tablespoon finely chopped ginger
1 teaspoon five-spice
½ teaspoon ground white pepper
3 tablespoons fish sauce
3 tablespoons kecap manis
2 tablespoons light soy sauce
35 g (1¼ oz/¼ cup) shaved palm
   sugar (jaggery)
1 small handful coriander
   (cilantro) leaves, chopped
100 g (3½ oz) mangetout (snow
   peas), thinly sliced

Note: Kecap manis is a thick, sweet soy sauce that is readily available in Asian grocers and good supermarkets.

1. Cut the spare ribs into 2.5 cm (1 in) thick pieces, discarding any small pieces of bone. Put into a saucepan and cover with cold water. Bring to the boil then reduce to a simmer and cook for 5 minutes. Drain and set aside.

2. Heat the oil in a heavy-based saucepan over medium–high heat. Add the pork and garlic and stir until lightly browned. Add remaining ingredients except mangetout, plus 560 ml (19¼ fl oz/2¼ cups) water. Cover, bring to the boil then reduce to a simmer and cook, stirring occasionally, for 15–18 minutes, or until the pork is tender. Stir in the mangetout and serve.

five-spice

Five-spice originated in China, though it is now used in many parts of Southeast Asia. It contains ground star anise, fennel seeds, cassia or cinnamon, Szechuan pepper and cloves. As with all spice blends, proportions vary depending on the cook, though generally the star anise dominates. In some versions, five-spice is not five at all but six- or seven-spice — ginger and/or cardamom may sneak in. This blend is pungent and quite potent, so a little goes a long way. It is used in marinades for meat, fish or poultry — its most famous use is in the marinade for Peking duck — and also with vegetables, in stir-fries and even on fruit.

Barbecued duck curry with lychees

SERVES 4 * **PREPARATION TIME: 20 MINUTES** * **COOKING TIME: 25 MINUTES**

This colourful curry features the delicate appeal of lychees. Native to China but now grown in Southeast Asia and India, lychees have a creamy, sweet flesh and gentle perfume. The spice paste is earthy and peppery, rather than hot, and balances well with the rich-tasting meat and coconut.

Curry paste

1 teaspoon white peppercorns
1 teaspoon shrimp paste
3 long red chillies, seeded
1 red onion, roughly chopped
2 garlic cloves
2 lemon grass stems, white part only, thinly sliced
5 cm (2 in) piece ginger
3 coriander (cilantro) roots
5 kaffir lime (makrut) leaves
2 tablespoons oil
2 teaspoons ground coriander
1 teaspoon ground cumin
1 teaspoon paprika
1 teaspoon ground turmeric

1 Chinese barbecued duck
400 ml (14 fl oz) coconut cream
1 tablespoon shaved palm sugar (jaggery)
2 tablespoons fish sauce
1 thick slice galangal
240 g (8½ oz) tinned straw mushrooms, drained
400 g (14 oz) tinned lychees, cut in half (reserve 60 ml/2 fl oz/¼ cup syrup)
250 g (9 oz) cherry tomatoes
1 handful Thai basil, chopped
1 handful leaves coriander (cilantro), chopped

Note: When in season, you can use fresh lychees, which will be sweeter and juicier than the tinned variety so you won't need the added syrup.

1. Dry-fry the peppercorns and the shrimp paste wrapped in some foil in a frying pan over medium–high heat for 2–3 minutes, or until fragrant. Allow to cool. Using a mortar with a pestle, or a spice grinder, crush or grind the peppercorns to a powder. Put the crushed peppercorns and the shrimp with the remaining curry paste ingredients in a food processor, or in a mortar with a pestle, and process or pound to a smooth paste.

2. Remove the duck meat from the bones and chop into bite-sized pieces. Put the thick coconut cream from the top of the tin in a saucepan, bring to a rapid simmer over medium heat, stirring occasionally, and cook for 5–10 minutes, or until the mixture 'splits' (the oil starts to separate). Add half the curry paste, palm sugar and fish sauce and stir until the palm sugar is dissolved. Add the duck, galangal, straw mushrooms, lychees, reserved lychee syrup and remaining coconut cream. Bring to the boil then reduce to a simmer and cook for 15–20 minutes, or until the duck is tender.

3. Add the cherry tomatoes, basil and coriander. Season to taste. Serve when the cherry tomatoes are slightly softened.

Process all the curry paste ingredients until smooth.

Remove the duck meat from the bones and chop.

Beef balls with pickled garlic

SERVES 4 ✳ **PREPARATION TIME: 20 MINUTES** ✳ **COOKING TIME: 25 MINUTES**

This dish involves little preparation, making it a welcome choice when you feel like a curry but can't be bothered with the grinding and roasting. Pickled garlic has a sweet–sour flavour and is used in curries as a means of balancing other flavours — be they hot, creamy or sweet.

Meatballs
450 g (1 lb) minced (ground) beef
3 garlic cloves, crushed
1 teaspoon white pepper
1 small handful leaves coriander
    (cilantro), chopped
1 small handful Thai basil, chopped
1 spring onion (scallion),
    finely chopped
3 teaspoons fish sauce
1 egg

3 tablespoons oil
3 tablespoons green curry paste,
    ready-made or see recipe on
    page 100
3 tablespoons finely chopped ginger
1½ teaspoons ground turmeric
3 tablespoons fish sauce
3 kaffir lime (makrut) leaves
2½ tablespoons tamarind purée
3 tablespoons chopped pickled garlic
1½ tablespoons shaved palm sugar
    (jaggery)

1. To make the meatballs, combine all the ingredients together well. Then, taking a tablespoon at a time, roll the mixture into small balls. You should have about 24 balls.

2. Heat the oil in a heavy-based saucepan over medium heat and add the curry paste, ginger and turmeric and cook, stirring frequently for about 5 minutes, or until fragrant.

3. Add the fish sauce, kaffir lime leaves and tamarind. Bring to the boil then cover, reduce to a simmer and cook for 5 minutes. Add the meatballs, pickled garlic and palm sugar and simmer for 15 minutes, or until meatballs are cooked through.

Roll tablespoons of the mince mixture into 24 balls.

Add the meatballs to the sauce and simmer until cooked through.

15 mins

Chicken and Thai apple aubergine curry

SERVES 4 * **PREPARATION TIME: 15 MINUTES** * **COOKING TIME: 25 MINUTES**

This savoury curry has lots of flavour and is well balanced. Thai apple aubergines (eggplant) can be a bit of an acquired taste. When fresh, they are crisp and clean and almost sweet tasting, but when old and musty, become quite bitter.

Curry paste
1 teaspoon white peppercorns
2 tablespoons dried shrimp
1 teaspoon shrimp paste
2 tablespoons chopped coriander
(cilantro) root
3 lemon grass stems, white part
only, thinly sliced
3 garlic cloves
1 tablespoon finely chopped ginger
1 red chilli, chopped
4 kaffir lime (makrut) leaves
3 tablespoons fish sauce
3 tablespoons lime juice
1 teaspoon ground turmeric

500 g (1 lb 2 oz) chicken thigh fillets
250 g (9 oz) Thai apple aubergine
(eggplant)
400 ml (14 fl oz) coconut cream
(do not shake the tin)
2 tablespoons shaved palm sugar
(jaggery)
1 red pepper (capsicum), sliced
230 g (8½ oz) tinned water
chestnuts, drained and sliced
1 tablespoon chopped coriander
(cilantro) leaves
1 tablespoon chopped Thai basil

Note: Thai apple aubergines are available from Asian food stores over summer and into early autumn. Baby aubergines can be used in place of Thai apple aubergines.

1. Dry-fry the peppercorns, dried shrimp and the shrimp paste wrapped in some foil in a frying pan over medium–high heat for 2–3 minutes, or until fragrant. Allow to cool. Using a mortar with a pestle, or a spice grinder, crush or grind the peppercorns to a powder. Process the dried shrimp in a food processor until it becomes very finely shredded.

2. Put the crushed peppercorns, shredded dried shrimp and the shrimp paste with the remaining curry paste ingredients in a food processor, or in a mortar with a pestle, and process or pound to a smooth paste. Cut the chicken thigh fillets into 2.5 cm (1 in) cubes. Cut the aubergine into pieces of a similar size.

3. Put the thick coconut cream from the top of the tin in a saucepan, bring to a rapid simmer over medium heat, stirring occasionally, and cook for 5–10 minutes, or until the mixture 'splits' (the oil starts to separate). Add the curry paste and stir for 5–6 minutes, or until fragrant. Add the palm sugar and stir until dissolved. Add the chicken, aubergine, pepper, half the remaining coconut cream and the water chestnuts. Bring to the boil, cover and reduce to a simmer and cook for 15 minutes, or until the chicken is cooked and aubergine soft. Stir in the remaining coconut cream, coriander and basil.

Finely grind the peppercorns in a mortar or use a spice grinder.

Cut the aubergine into pieces similar in size to the chicken.

Three ways with bread

A curry served on its own is no curry at all. Rice, side dishes of raitas or chutneys and breads such as naan are what makes them complete. Furthermore, it's a rare curry that does not happily lend itself to being scooped up with some bread. Here are three classic choices: dry, unleavened rotis and chapatis, the basic everyday breads of India; and soft, oven-baked naan, which are leavened with a starter to give them their puffed appearance.

Roti

MAKES 12 * **PREPARATION TIME: 20 MINUTES** * **COOKING TIME: 15 MINUTES**

Sift 375 g (13 oz/3 cups) roti or plain (all-purpose) flour into a large mixing bowl with 1 teaspoon salt. Rub in 2 tablespoons softened ghee or oil with your fingertips. Add 1 lightly beaten egg and 250 ml (9 fl oz/1 cup) warm water, and mix together with a flat-bladed knife to form a moist dough. Turn out on to a well-floured surface and knead for 10 minutes, or until you have a soft dough. Sprinkle with more flour as necessary. Form the dough into a ball and brush with oil. Place in a bowl, cover and rest for 2 hours. Working on a lightly-floured bench top, divide the dough into 12 pieces and roll into even-sized balls. Take one ball and, working with a little oil on your fingertips, hold the ball in the air and work around the edge pulling out the dough until a 2 mm x 15 cm (¹⁄₁₆ x 6 in) round is formed. Lay on a lightly-floured surface and cover with plastic wrap so that it doesn't dry out. Repeat the process with the remaining balls. Heat a large frying pan over high heat and brush it with ghee or oil. Carefully place one roti in the frying pan, brush with some extra beaten egg and cook for 1 minute, or until the underside is golden. Slide onto a plate and brush the pan with some more ghee or oil. Cook the other side of the roti for 50–60 seconds, or until golden. Remove from the pan and cover to keep warm. Cook the remaining rotis in the same way.

Chapati

MAKES 14 * **PREPARATION TIME: 20 MINUTES** * **COOKING TIME: 20 MINUTES**

Put 280 g (10 oz/2¼ cups) atta (chapati) flour in a large bowl with a pinch of salt. Slowly add 250 ml (9 fl oz/1 cup) water, or enough to form a firm dough. Put on a lightly floured surface and knead until smooth. Cover with plastic wrap and leave for 50 minutes. Divide into 14 portions and roll into 14 cm (5½ in) circles. Heat a frying pan over medium heat and brush with melted ghee or oil. Cook the chapatis one at a time, flattening the surface, for 2–3 minutes on each side, or until golden brown and bubbles appear.

Naan

MAKES 8 * **PREPARATION TIME: 15 MINUTES + RESTING** * **COOKING TIME: 10 MINUTES**

Preheat the oven to 200°C (400°F/Gas 6). Lightly grease two 28 x 32 cm (11¼ x 12¾ in) baking trays. Sift together 500 g (1 lb 2 oz/4 cups) plain (all-purpose) flour, 1 teaspoon baking powder, ½ teaspoon bicarbonate of soda (baking soda) and 1 teaspoon salt. Mix in 1 beaten egg, 1 tablespoon melted ghee or butter, 125 g (4½ oz/½ cup) plain yoghurt and gradually add enough milk to form a soft dough — about 250 ml (9 fl oz/1 cup). Cover with a damp cloth and leave in a warm place for 2 hours. Knead the dough on a well-floured surface for 2–3 minutes, or until smooth. Divide into 8 portions and roll each one into an oval 15 cm (6 in) long. Brush with water and place, wet side down, on the prepared baking trays. Brush with melted ghee or butter and bake for 8–10 minutes, or until golden brown. To make garlic naan, crush 6 garlic cloves and sprinkle evenly over the dough prior to baking.

15 mins

Sour lamb and bamboo curry

SERVES 4 * **PREPARATION TIME: 15 MINUTES** * **COOKING TIME: 30 MINUTES**

Bamboo shoots are used mainly in Southeast Asian cooking. When fresh, they have a lovely crisp, nutty bitterness to them. They are available in Asian food stores, but the tinned variety makes an acceptable substitute. Along with the green beans and lamb, they provide texture to this curry.

Curry paste
1 teaspoon white peppercorns
1 teaspoon shrimp paste
30 g (1 oz) dried shrimp
6 spring onions (scallions), sliced
60 g (2¼ oz) jalapeño chillies
 (in brine), sliced
2 lemon grass stems, white part
 only, thinly sliced
6 garlic cloves, crushed
4 coriander (cilantro) roots, chopped
2 teaspoons ground galangal
1 teaspoon chilli powder
80 ml (2½ fl oz/⅓ cup) fish sauce
80 ml (2½ fl oz/⅓ cup) lime juice
1 teaspoon ground turmeric

500 g (1 lb 2 oz) boneless lamb leg,
 trimmed of excess fat
1 tablespoon oil
1 tablespoon shaved palm sugar
 (jaggery)
250 ml (9 fl oz/1 cup) coconut
 cream
60 g (2¼ oz/¼ cup) tamarind purée
1½ tablespoons fish sauce
400 g (14 oz) tinned bamboo shoot
 pieces, cut into thick wedges
200 g (7 oz) green beans, cut into
 4 cm (1½ in) lengths

Note: Jalapeño chillies in brine are available from Spanish grocers and supermarkets, and are sometimes called guindillas. If neccesssary, 20 g of fresh jalapeño chillies can be used in place of 60 g in brine.

1. Dry-fry the peppercorns and the shrimp paste wrapped in some foil in a frying pan over medium–high heat for 2–3 minutes, or until fragrant. Allow to cool. Using a mortar with a pestle, or a spice grinder, crush or grind to a powder. Process the dried shrimp in a food processor until it becomes very finely shredded.

2. Put the crushed peppercorns, shrimp paste and dried shrimp with the remaining curry paste ingredients in a food processor, or in a mortar with a pestle, and process or pound to a smooth paste.

3. Slice the lamb into strips 5 x 2 cm (2 x ¾ in) and 3 mm (⅛ in) thick. Heat the oil in a heavy-based casserole dish over medium heat and add 2–3 tablespoons of paste. Stir constantly, adding the palm sugar. When the palm sugar has dissolved add the lamb, stirring for about 7 minutes, or until lightly golden.

4. Add the coconut cream, 250 ml (9 fl oz/1 cup) water, tamarind, fish sauce and bamboo. Bring to the boil then reduce heat and simmer for about 20 minutes, or until tender. Add the beans and simmer for a further 3 minutes. Season to taste and serve.

20 mins

Malaysian nonya chicken curry

SERVES 4 ✳ PREPARATION TIME: 20 MINUTES ✳ COOKING TIME: 25 MINUTES

In the fifteenth century, the Strait of Malacca was the favoured route of Chinese traders to Arabia and India. Many settled in the area and married the local women, who became known as 'nonya'. A unique cuisine developed, which blended Chinese techniques and Malaysian spices.

Curry paste
½ teaspoon shrimp paste
2 red onions, chopped
4 red chillies, seeded
4 garlic cloves, crushed
2 lemon grass stems, white part only, sliced
3 cm (1¼ in) cube galangal, sliced
8 kaffir lime (makrut) leaves, roughly chopped
1 teaspoon ground turmeric

2 tablespoons oil
750 g (1 lb 10 oz) chicken thigh fillets, cut into bite-sized pieces
400 ml (14 fl oz) coconut milk
3½ tablespoons tamarind purée
1 tablespoon fish sauce
3 kaffir lime (makrut) leaves, shredded

1. Dry-fry the shrimp paste wrapped in some foil in a frying pan over medium–high heat for 2–3 minutes, or until fragrant. Allow to cool.

2. Put the shrimp paste with the remaining curry paste ingredients in a food processor, or in a mortar with a pestle, and process or pound to a smooth paste. Heat a wok or large saucepan over high heat, add the oil and swirl to coat the side. Add the curry paste and cook, stirring occasionally, over low heat for 8–10 minutes, or until fragrant. Add the chicken and stir-fry with the paste for 2–3 minutes.

3. Add the coconut milk, tamarind purée and fish sauce to the wok, and simmer, stirring occasionally, for 15–20 minutes, or until the chicken is tender. Garnish with the shredded kaffir lime leaves and serve.

Put the paste ingredients in a food processor or mortar.

Process or pound the mixture until a smooth paste is formed.

Thai sweet pork and pineapple curry

SERVES 4 * **PREPARATION TIME: 20 MINUTES** * **COOKING TIME: 20 MINUTES**

This refreshing curry is a vibrant mix of fresh ingredients — pineapple, tomatoes, cucumber and coriander (cilantro) — and sweet–sour seasonings such as vinegar and palm sugar. This combination makes it a great summer dish: it has a refreshing, slightly spicy and sweet flavour.

500 g (1 lb 2 oz) boneless pork leg, trimmed of excess fat

1 tablespoon oil

3 garlic cloves, crushed

125 ml (4 fl oz/½ cup) brown malt vinegar

45 g (1½ oz/¼ cup) shaved palm sugar (jaggery)

3 tablespoons tomato purée (paste)

1 tomato, cut into wedges

1 onion, cut into thin wedges

90 g (3¼ oz/½ cup) pineapple, cut into chunks

½ cucumber, halved lengthways, seeded and sliced

½ red pepper (capsicum), cut into strips

2½ tablespoons jalapeño chillies (in brine), chopped

2 spring onions (scallions), cut into 5 cm (2 in) pieces

1 small handful coriander (cilantro) leaves

1. Cut the pork into 3 cm (1¼ in) cubes. Heat the oil in a large saucepan over medium heat. Add the pork and garlic and cook for 4–5 minutes, or until pork is lightly browned.

2. In another saucepan, stir the vinegar, palm sugar, ½ teaspoon salt and the tomato purée over medium heat for 3 minutes, or until the palm sugar is dissolved.

3. Add the vinegar mixture to the pork along with the tomato, onion, pineapple, cucumber, pepper, and jalapeños. Bring to the boil then reduce to a simmer and cook for 8–10 minutes, or until the pork is tender. Stir in the spring onions and coriander and serve.

Trim the pork fillet of excess fat and cut into neat cubes.

Add the cucumber and red pepper to the saucepan.

Rich chicken koftas

SERVES 4 * **PREPARATION TIME: 20 MINUTES** * **COOKING TIME: 30 MINUTES**

Kofta might contain meat, fish or vegetables but all are well-combined mixtures, with added herbs and spices. Accompanying sauces are equally appealing — in this dish, the sauce is rich with coconut, yoghurt, cream and almonds, balanced by the spicy, peppery notes of garam masala and turmeric.

Mix the chicken, onion mixture, coriander and salt together.

Use wetted hands to shape the chicken mixture into balls.

Koftas

2 tablespoons oil
1 onion, finely chopped
1 garlic clove, crushed
1 teaspoon finely chopped ginger
1 teaspoon ground cumin
1 teaspoon garam masala
½ teaspoon ground turmeric
650 g (1 lb 7 oz) chicken thigh
    fillets, trimmed
2 tablespoons chopped coriander
    (cilantro) leaves

1 onion, roughly chopped
1 tablespoon ghee or oil
2 garlic cloves, crushed
2 teaspoons garam masala
½ teaspoon ground turmeric
170 ml (5½ fl oz/⅔ cup)
    coconut milk
90 g (3¼ oz/⅓ cup) plain yoghurt
125 ml (4 fl oz/½ cup) cream
    (whipping)
35 g (1¼ oz/⅓ cup) ground almonds
2 tablespoons chopped coriander
    (cilantro) leaves

1. To make the koftas, heat half the oil in a frying pan. Add the onion, garlic, ginger, ground cumin, garam masala and ground turmeric, and cook, stirring, for 4–6 minutes, or until the onion is tender and spices are fragrant. Allow to cool.

2. Put the chicken fillets in batches in a food processor and process until just chopped. Do not over-process the mixture. Put the chicken, onion mixture, coriander and ½ teaspoon salt in a bowl, and mix together well. Using wetted hands, measure 1 tablespoon of mixture and shape into a ball. Repeat with the remaining mixture. Heat the remaining oil in a heavy-based frying pan, add the koftas in batches and cook for 4–5 minutes, or until well browned all over. Remove from the pan and cover. Put the onion in a food processor and process until smooth.

3. Heat the ghee or oil in a frying pan. Add the onion and garlic, and cook, stirring, for 5 minutes, or until the onion juices evaporate and the mixture starts to thicken. Add the garam masala and turmeric, and cook for a further 2 minutes. Add the coconut milk, yoghurt, cream and ground almonds. Gently bring almost to the boil, then reduce the heat to medium and add the koftas. Cook, stirring occasionally, for 15 minutes, or until the koftas are cooked through. Stir in the coriander and serve.

15 mins

Thai red duck curry with pineapple

SERVES 4–6 ＊ **PREPARATION TIME: 15 MINUTES** ＊ **COOKING TIME: 15 MINUTES**

The art of Thai curries — and the reason why we keep coming back to them — is the way they combine different flavours and textures in the one dish to create a harmonious whole. This dish is a perfect example of that skill; blending sweet, savoury and spicy ingredients with rich coconut milk.

Red curry paste
15 dried long red chillies
1 tablespoon white peppercorns
2 teaspoons coriander seeds
1 teaspoon cumin seeds
2 teaspoons shrimp paste
5 red Asian shallots, chopped
10 garlic cloves, chopped
2 lemon grass stems, white part only, finely sliced
1 tablespoon chopped galangal
2 tablespoons chopped coriander (cilantro) root
1 teaspoon finely grated kaffir lime (makrut) zest

1 tablespoon peanut oil
8 spring onions (scallions), sliced on the diagonal into 3 cm (1¼ in) lengths
2 garlic cloves, crushed
1 Chinese roast duck, chopped into large pieces
400 ml (14 fl oz) coconut milk
450 g (1 lb) pineapple pieces in syrup, tinned and drained
3 kaffir lime (makrut) leaves
3 tablespoons chopped coriander (cilantro) leaves
2 tablespoons chopped mint

1. Soak the chillies in boiling water for 5 minutes, or until soft. Remove the stem and seeds, then chop. Dry-fry the peppercorns, coriander seeds, cumin seeds, and shrimp paste wrapped in foil in a frying pan over medium–high heat for 2–3 minutes, or until fragrant. Allow to cool. Using a mortar with a pestle, or a spice grinder, crush or grind the peppercorns, coriander and cumin to a powder.

2. Put the chopped chillies, shrimp paste and ground spices with the remaining curry paste ingredients in a food processor, or in a mortar with a pestle, and process or pound to a smooth paste.

3. Heat a wok until very hot, add the oil and swirl to coat the side. Add the onion, garlic and 2–4 tablespoons made red curry paste, and stir-fry for 1 minute, or until fragrant.

4. Add the roast duck pieces, coconut milk, drained pineapple pieces, kaffir lime leaves, and half the coriander and mint. Bring to the boil, then reduce the heat and simmer for 10 minutes, or until the duck is heated through and the sauce has thickened slightly. Stir in the remaining coriander and mint, and serve.

Pork and cardamom curry

SERVES 6 ✳ **PREPARATION TIME: 10 MINUTES** ✳ **COOKING TIME: 30 MINUTES**

Tender, sweet pork fillet is perfect for this dish: it is fat-free, so needs an initial brief cooking to seal in the juices, but then will cook fairly quickly in the curry. The spices — peppercorns, ginger, cardamom, cumin, garam masala — combine to give this dish a lovely warm, exotic flavour.

Curry paste
10 cardamom pods
6 cm (2½ in) piece ginger, chopped
3 garlic cloves, crushed
2 teaspoons black peppercorns
1 cinnamon stick
1 onion, finely sliced
1 teaspoon ground cumin
1 teaspoon ground coriander
1 teaspoon garam masala

3 tablespoons oil
1 kg (2 lb 4 oz) pork fillet,
   thinly sliced
2 tomatoes, finely diced
125 ml (4 fl oz/½ cup) chicken stock
125 ml (4 fl oz/½ cup) coconut milk

1. Lightly crush the cardamom pods with the flat side of a heavy knife. Remove the seeds, discarding the pods. Put the seeds and the remaining curry paste ingredients in a food processor, or in a mortar with a pestle, and process or pound to a smooth paste.

2. Put 2½ tablespoons of oil in a large heavy-based frying pan, and fry the pork in batches until browned, then set aside. Add the remaining oil to the pan, then add the curry paste and cook over medium–high heat for 3–4 minutes, or until aromatic. Add the tomato, chicken stock and coconut milk, and simmer covered over low–medium heat for 15 minutes. While cooking, skim any oil that comes to the surface and discard.

3. Add the pork to the sauce, and simmer uncovered for 5 minutes, or until cooked. Season well to taste and serve.

cardamom

Warm and pungent, with lemony undertones, cardamom has been chewed as a breath freshener from the time of the ancient Egyptians to today. Many varieties of cardamom are grown, but the smooth green pods from their native southern India and Sri Lanka are considered the best. Also of note are the large, wrinkled black (brown) pods, which have a coarser flavour. Green cardamom is difficult to harvest, making it expensive and highly valued. It is used in both sweet and savoury Indian and Asian dishes, and both black and green cardamom are essential components of garam masala. Green cardamom is sometimes bleached to form white cardamom.

Thai green chicken curry

SERVES 4–6 ✳ **PREPARATION TIME: 20 MINUTES** ✳ **COOKING TIME: 30 MINUTES**

This dish is a classic of Thai cooking. It is hot and fragrant from the curry paste and perfumed with kaffir lime (makrut) leaves and Thai basil. Green pastes can vary, but they should be pungent rather than piercingly hot, and built around chillies, galangal, coriander (cilantro) and lemon grass.

Green curry paste
1 teaspoon white peppercorns
2 tablespoons coriander seeds
1 teaspoon cumin seeds
2 teaspoons shrimp paste
1 teaspoon sea salt
4 lemon grass stems, white part
   only, finely sliced
2 teaspoons chopped galangal
1 kaffir lime (makrut) leaf,
   finely shredded
1 tablespoon chopped coriander
   (cilantro) root
5 red Asian shallots, chopped
10 garlic cloves, crushed
16 long green chillies, seeded
   and chopped

500 ml (17 fl oz/2 cups) coconut
   cream (do not shake the tins)
2 tablespoons shaved palm sugar
   (jaggery)
2 tablespoons fish sauce
4 kaffir lime (makrut) leaves,
   finely shredded
1 kg (2 lb 4 oz) chicken thigh or
   breast fillets, cut into thick strips
200 g (7 oz) bamboo shoots, cut
   into thick strips
100 g (3½ oz) yard-long (snake)
   beans, cut into 5 cm (2 in) lengths
1 handful Thai basil

1. Dry-fry the peppercorns, coriander seeds, cumin seeds and shrimp paste wrapped in foil in a frying pan over medium–high heat for 2–3 minutes, or until fragrant. Allow to cool. Using a mortar with a pestle, or a spice grinder, crush or grind the peppercorns, coriander and cumin to a powder.

2. Put the shrimp paste and ground spices with the remaining curry paste ingredients in a food processor, or in a mortar with a pestle, and process or pound to a smooth paste.

3. Put the thick coconut cream from the top of the tins in a saucepan, bring to a rapid simmer over medium heat, stirring occasionally, and cook for 5–10 minutes, or until the mixture 'splits' (the oil starts to separate).

4. Add 4 tablespoons of the made green curry paste, then simmer for 10 minutes, or until fragrant. Add the palm sugar, fish sauce and kaffir lime leaves to the pan.

5. Stir in the remaining coconut cream and the chicken, bamboo shoots and beans, and simmer for 15 minutes, or until the chicken is tender. Stir in the Thai basil and serve.

Lift off the thick coconut cream from the top of the tins.

Cook the curry paste in the coconut cream until oily.

Rogan josh

SERVES 6 * **PREPARATION TIME: 15 MINUTES + MARINATING TIME**
COOKING TIME: 50 MINUTES

This classic, superbly aromatic, slow-cooking curry originated in Persia, and travelled to Kashmir, in India's far north, under the Moghul empire. In Kashmir it was adapted and perfected, incorporating the local chillies, saffron and cardamom.

8 garlic cloves, crushed
3 teaspoons grated ginger
2 teaspoons ground cumin
1 teaspoon chilli powder
2 teaspoons paprika
2 teaspoons ground coriander
1 kg (2 lb 4 oz) boneless leg
  or shoulder of lamb, cut into
  3 cm (1¼ in) cubes
3 tablespoons ghee or oil
1 onion, finely chopped
6 cardamom pods, bruised
4 cloves
2 Indian bay (cassia) leaves
1 cinnamon stick
185 g (6½ oz/¾ cup) Greek-style
  yoghurt
4 saffron threads, mixed with
  2 tablespoons milk
¼ teaspoon garam masala

Note: Indian bay leaves can be found in Asian Grocers. If necessary, 1 bay leaf can be used in place of every 2 Indian bay leaves.

1. Mix the garlic, ginger, cumin, chilli powder, paprika and coriander in a large bowl. Add the meat and stir thoroughly to coat the meat cubes well. Cover and marinate for at least 2 hours, or overnight, in the refrigerator.

2. Heat the ghee or oil in a flameproof casserole dish or karahi over medium-high heat. Add the cardamom pods, cloves, bay leaves and cinnamon to the dish and fry for 1 minute. Increase the heat to high, add the meat and onion, then mix well and fry for 2 minutes. Stir well, then reduce the heat to low, cover and cook for 10 minutes. Uncover and fry for another 2 minutes, or until the meat is quite dry. Add 100 ml (3½ fl oz) water, cover and cook for 4 minutes, until the water has evaporated and the oil separates out and floats on the surface. Fry the meat for another 1–2 minutes, then add 250 ml (9 fl oz/1 cup) water. Cover and cook for 30–40 minutes, gently simmering until the meat is tender. The liquid will reduce quite a bit.

3. Stir in the yoghurt when the meat is almost tender, taking care not to allow the meat to catch on the base of the dish. Add the saffron and milk. Stir the mixture a few times to mix in the saffron. Season with salt to taste. Remove from the heat and sprinkle with the garam masala.

Coat the meat well in the mixed spices and leave to marinate.

Dry-fry the spices for 1 minute, or until they become aromatic.

Chicken curry with apricots

SERVES 6–8 ✳ **PREPARATION TIME: 15 MINUTES** ✳ **COOKING TIME: 45 MINUTES**

This dish is a lovely blend of sweet, rich apricots and mellow, round spices such as cumin, turmeric and cardamom. With fresh ginger and green chillies providing a bit of bite, the chicken itself seems like an almost incidental ingredient!

18 dried 'Ready-to-eat' apricots
1 tablespoon ghee or oil
2 x 1.5 kg (3 lb 5 oz) chickens, jointed
3 onions, finely sliced
1 teaspoon grated ginger
3 garlic cloves, crushed
3 long green chillies, seeded and finely chopped
1 teaspoon cumin seeds
1 teaspoon chilli powder
½ teaspoon ground turmeric
4 cardamom pods, bruised
4 large tomatoes, peeled and cut into eight pieces

1. Melt the ghee or add the oil to a large saucepan, add the chicken in batches and cook over high heat for 4–5 minutes, or until browned. Remove from the pan. Add the onion, ginger, garlic and chopped green chilli, and cook, stirring often, for 5 minutes, or until the onion has softened and turned golden brown. Stir in the cumin seeds, chilli powder and ground turmeric, and cook for a further 1 minute.

2. Return the chicken to the pan, add the cardamom, tomato and apricots, with any remaining liquid, and mix well. Simmer, covered, for 30 minutes, or until the chicken is tender.

Sauté the chicken pieces in batches until browned.

Stir the spices into the onion mixture and cook until fragrant.

10 mins

Balti-style lamb

SERVES 4 * **PREPARATION TIME: 10 MINUTES** * **COOKING TIME: 55 MINUTES**

Baltistan may lie high in the mountains of north Pakistan, but Birmingham, England, has become the international launch pad of balti cuisine. Distinctive for its use of the two-handled karahi pot, it also features its own masala paste, which is herby and fragrant with green cardamom.

1 kg (2 lb 4 oz) lamb leg steaks, cut into 3 cm (1¼ in) cubes
5 tablespoons ready-made balti masala paste
2 tablespoons ghee or oil
3 garlic cloves, crushed
1 tablespoon garam masala
1 large onion, finely chopped
2 tablespoons chopped coriander (cilantro) leaves, plus extra for garnish

1. Preheat the oven to 190°C (375°F/Gas 5). Put the meat, 1 tablespoon of the balti masala paste and 375 ml (13 fl oz/1½ cups) boiling water in a large casserole dish or karahi, and combine. Cook, covered, in the oven for 30 minutes, or until almost cooked through. Drain, reserving the stock.

2. Meanwhile heat the ghee or oil in a wok, add the garlic and garam masala, and stir-fry over medium heat for 1 minute. Add the onion and cook for 5 minutes, or until the onion is soft and golden brown. Set aside until lamb is cooked. Then increase the heat, add the remaining balti masala paste and the lamb. Cook for 5 minutes to brown the meat. Slowly add the reserved stock and simmer over low heat, stirring occasionally, for 10 minutes.

3. Add the chopped coriander leaves and 185 ml (6 fl oz/¾ cup) water and simmer for 10 minutes, or until the meat is tender and the sauce has thickened slightly. Season with salt and freshly ground black pepper and garnish with extra coriander leaves.

ghee

Ghee is most often associated with Indian cooking, but its usefulness as a cooking medium means it is now used throughout Southeast Asia. It is a clarified butter — that is, butter that has been melted and boiled to remove milk solids and water. The resulting ghee has a high burning point, little moisture and a high fat content, so a little goes a long way. Most importantly, ghee has a strong nutty flavour and rich, toasted aroma, which is used to advantage in meat and vegetable curries, lentil dals and rice dishes. Buy from Asian and Indian food stores and store in a cool, dark place.

The perfect spice blend

A spice blend is a wonderful synergy of complementary spices. Whole spices — being the dried seeds, stems, bark or roots of particular plants — are dry-fried or roasted then finely ground to a powder to release their natural, aromatic oils. The most commonly known of these spice blends is curry powder. This mixture comes in several guises, forming the flavour structure for many curries, particularly Indian and Sri Lankan varieties. Although mainly used as the base flavour for cooked dishes, some spice blends, such as garam masala or five-spice, are often utilized at the end of the cooking process as a final aromatic addition to a dish.

For convenience, you will find most well-known spice blends in supermarkets and Asian food stores but, as with curry pastes, fresh is undoubtedly best. Fresh, whole spices retain many of the natural oils which carry flavour and aroma. If the spices are old or have been pre-ground for some time, they may have lost flavour due to age and exposure to air. So it is best to buy small amounts of whole spices and replace them as required.

To make your own spice blend, first dry-fry spices in a frying pan over medium–high heat for 2–3 minutes, or until fragrant. Ideally, dry-fry each spice separately to obtain optimum flavour as certain spices, depending on size and moisture content, will take longer than others to become fragrant. This process mellows the flavour of the spices, making for a well-rounded final result in your cooking. Allow the spices to cool then put them in a mortar and pound with a pestle until finely ground. You can also use a coffee or spice grinder. Store ground spices in a clean, well-sealed glass jar for up to 3 weeks, after which time the flavour will diminish rapidly.

Thai beef and squash curry

SERVES 6 * **PREPARATION TIME: 15 MINUTES** * **COOKING TIME: 1 HOUR**

Curries are as much about aroma as they are about taste, but this curry also contributes a wonderful tender texture to the mix. Soft, sweet butternut squash, moist, rich beef and crunchy peanuts come together in a sauce that is hot, rich and sweet.

Pour the coconut milk into the curry mixture and simmer.

2 tablespoons oil
750 g (1 lb 10 oz) braising (casserole) steak, thinly sliced
4 tablespoons ready-made musaman curry paste
2 garlic cloves, crushed
1 onion, sliced
6 curry leaves, torn
750 ml (26 fl oz/3 cups) coconut milk
450 g (1 lb/3 cups) butternut squash, roughly diced
2 tablespoons, chopped raw peanuts
1 tablespoon shaved palm sugar (jaggery)
2 tablespoons tamarind purée
2 tablespoons fish sauce
curry leaves to serve

1. Heat a wok or frying pan over high heat. Add the oil and swirl to coat the sides. Add the meat in batches and cook for 5 minutes, or until browned. Remove the meat from the wok.

2. Add the curry paste, garlic, onion and curry leaves to the wok, and stir to coat. Return the meat to the wok and cook, stirring, over medium heat for 2 minutes.

3. Add the coconut milk to the wok, then reduce the heat and simmer for 30 minutes. Add the diced squash and simmer for 25–30 minutes, or until the meat and the squash are tender and the sauce has thickened.

4. Stir in the peanuts, palm sugar, tamarind purée and fish sauce, and simmer for 1 minute. Garnish with curry leaves and serve.

Add the squash and simmer until tender and sauce thickens.

15 mins

Minced lamb with orange

SERVES 6 ✳ **PREPARATION TIME: 15 MINUTES** ✳ **COOKING TIME: 1 HOUR**

There is probably no meat more versatile than lamb. This non-traditional curry blends aromatic ground spices with the sweetness of orange juice and the cleansing freshness of green chillies and mint. It is a thick, wet curry, ideal for serving with bread for mopping up any leftovers.

3 tablespoons oil
2 onions, finely diced
4 garlic cloves, crushed
3 teaspoons finely grated ginger
2 teaspoons ground cumin
2 teaspoons ground coriander
½ teaspoon ground turmeric
½ teaspoon cayenne pepper
1 teaspoon garam masala
1 kg (2 lb 4 oz) minced (ground) lamb
90 g (3¼ oz/⅓ cup) plain yoghurt
250 ml (9 fl oz/1 cup) orange juice
2 teaspoons orange zest
1 bay leaf
1 long green chilli, seeded and finely sliced
1 handful coriander (cilantro) leaves, roughly chopped
1 handful mint, roughly chopped

1. Heat the oil in a large heavy-based frying pan over medium heat. Add the onions, garlic, ginger and sauté for 5 minutes. Add the cumin, coriander, turmeric, cayenne pepper and garam masala, and cook for a further 5 minutes.

2. Increase the heat to high, add the lamb mince, and cook, stirring constantly to break the meat up. Add the yoghurt, a tablespoon at a time, stirring so that it combines well. Add the orange juice, zest, and bay leaf.

3. Bring to the boil then reduce to a simmer, cover and cook for 45 minutes, or until tender. While cooking, skim any oil that comes to the surface and discard. Season well to taste then stir through the green chilli, coriander and mint before serving.

coriander

Native to southern Europe and the Mediterranean, coriander (cilantro) is nevertheless an essential element in curries. Fresh and dried coriander are quite different, and of the fresh plant, the leaves, stem and root can all be used. The roots are used in curry pastes and sauces: the stems when a strong coriander flavour is needed, and the leaves are added at the end of cooking, for flavouring and to garnish. Fresh coriander is fragrant with a gingery edge, while the dried seeds have a sweeter, slightly peppery aroma. The flavour and aroma of the whole seeds are enhanced if they are lightly dry-fried before crushing.

15 mins

Sri Lankan fried pork curry

SERVES 6 ＊ **PREPARATION TIME: 15 MINUTES** ＊ **COOKING TIME: 1 HOUR**

This curry is interesting for the number of flavourings not often seen in western dishes. Fenugreek seeds are small, hard and ochre-coloured. They are powerfully scented and have a bitter taste, though this softens on cooking.

80 ml (2½ fl oz/⅓ cup) oil
1.25 kg (2 lb 12 oz) boned
   pork shoulder, cut into
   3 cm (1¼ in) cubes
1 large red onion, finely chopped
3–4 garlic cloves, crushed
1 tablespoon grated ginger
10 curry leaves
½ teaspoon fenugreek seeds
½ teaspoon chilli powder
6 cardamom pods, bruised
2½ tablespoons Sri Lankan
   curry powder
1 tablespoon white vinegar
3 tablespoons tamarind concentrate
270 ml (9½ fl oz) coconut cream

Note: Sri Lankan curry powder is available from Asian grocers and good supermarkets. Regular curry powder can be used in place of Sri Lankan curry powder.

1. Heat half the oil in a large saucepan over high heat, add the meat and cook in batches for 5 minutes, or until well browned. Remove from the pan. Heat the remaining oil, add the onion, garlic, ginger, curry leaves, spices and curry powder and cook over medium heat for 5 minutes, or until onion is lightly browned. Stir in the vinegar and 1 teaspoon salt.

2. Return the browned meat to the pan, add the tamarind concentrate and 310 ml (10¾ fl oz/1¼ cups) water and simmer, covered, stirring occasionally, for 30–40 minutes, or until the meat is tender. Stir in the coconut cream and simmer, uncovered, for 10–15 minutes, or until the sauce has reduced and thickened a little. Serve immediately.

tamarind

The tropical tamarind tree is prized for its fruit pods, each containing a sticky, fleshy acidic pulp wrapped around small, shiny, dark-brown seeds. The tree is indigenous to east Africa but it flourishes wild in India where the pulp is greatly appreciated for its refreshing sweet–sour taste and fruity aroma. Across tropical Asia it serves as an excellent souring agent, and is used in soups, curries, chutneys, drinks and sweetmeats. In the West, its main use is in Worcestershire sauce. Tamarind is sold as a concentrated paste in jars, or in blocks or cakes that still contain the seeds. Store both in the refrigerator for up to 1 year.

15 mins

Thai basil, beef and green peppercorn curry

SERVES 4 ∗ **PREPARATION TIME: 15 MINUTES + MARINATING TIME**
COOKING TIME: 1¼ HOURS

There are two ingredients in this dish that make it distinctly Thai (three if we include the curry paste). The first is Thai basil, with its distinctive perfume and clean flavour. The second is pickled green peppercorns. They add a salty, vinegary, slightly sweet quality, without too much heat.

2 tablespoons grated ginger
2 garlic cloves, crushed
500 g (1 lb 2 oz) rump steak
250 ml (9 fl oz/1 cup) coconut
  cream
1 tablespoon yellow curry paste,
  ready-made or see recipe on
  page 14
80 ml (2½ fl oz/⅓ cup) fish sauce
60 g (2¼ oz/⅓ cup) shaved palm
  sugar (jaggery)
2 lemon grass stems, white part
  only, finely chopped
1 thick slice galangal
4 kaffir lime (makrut) leaves
2 tomatoes, cut into 2 cm (¾ in) dice
400 g (14 oz) tinned large bamboo
  pieces, drained, cut into
  small chunks
25 g (1 oz) Thai pickled green
  peppercorns, on the stem
2 tablespoons tamarind purée
1 large handful Thai basil, chopped

Note: Thai pickled green peppercorns are available from Chinese and Thai grocers. Green peppercorns in brine may be substituted for Thai pickled green peppercorns.

1. Crush the ginger and garlic to a rough pulp in a mortar with a pestle, or food processor. Cut the meat into strips 5 x 2 cm (2 x ¾ in) and 3 mm (1/8 in) thick. Toss the ginger and garlic paste together with the beef and marinate for 30 minutes.

2. Bring half the coconut cream to the boil in a heavy-based casserole dish over medium heat then reduce to a simmer. Stir in the yellow curry paste and cook for 3–5 minutes. Add the fish sauce and palm sugar and stir until sugar is dissolved.

3. Increase heat to high, add the remaining ingredients and 375 ml (13 fl oz/1½ cups) water and bring the curry to the boil then reduce to a simmer and cook uncovered for 1 hour, or until the beef is tender.

4. Check seasoning and correct by adding extra fish sauce or palm sugar if necessary. Stir through the remaining coconut cream and serve immediately.

Pound the ginger and garlic together to a rough pulp.

Stir in the yellow curry paste and cook until aromatic.

15 mins

Lamb dhansak

SERVES 6 * **PREPARATION TIME: 15 MINUTES + SOAKING TIME**
COOKING TIME: 1¼ HOURS

This sumptuous curry comes from the Parsees of West India, who emigrated there from Iran in the seventh century. It is striking for the number of different lentils used, as well as vegetables such as spinach, squash and aubergine (eggplant), various spices and tender lamb.

100 g (3½ oz/¾ cup) yellow lentils
2 teaspoons dried yellow
  mung beans
2 tablespoons dried chickpeas
3 tablespoons red lentils
1 aubergine (eggplant), unpeeled
150 g (5½ oz) butternut squash,
  unpeeled
2 tablespoons ghee or oil
1 onion, finely chopped
3 garlic cloves, crushed
1 tablespoon grated ginger
1 kg (2 lb 4 oz) boneless leg
  or shoulder of lamb, cut into
  3 cm (1¼ in) cubes
1 cinnamon stick
5 cardamom pods, bruised
3 cloves
1 tablespoon ground coriander
1 teaspoon ground turmeric
1 teaspoon chilli powder, or to taste
150 g (5½ oz) amaranth or spinach
  leaves, cut into
  5 cm (2 in) lengths
2 tomatoes, halved
2 long green chillies, split
  lengthways and seeded
3 tablespoons lime juice

1. Soak the yellow lentils, yellow mung beans and chickpeas in hot water for about 1 hour, then drain well.

2. Put all four types of pulse in a saucepan, add 1 litre (35 fl oz/4 cups) water, cover and bring to the boil. Uncover and simmer for 15 minutes, skimming off any scum that forms on the surface, and stirring occasionally to make sure all the pulses are cooking at the same rate and are soft. Drain the pulses and lightly mash to a similar texture.

3. Meanwhile, cook the aubergine and squash in boiling water for 10–15 minutes, or until soft. Scoop out the squash flesh and cut it into pieces. Peel the aubergine carefully (it may be very pulpy) and cut the flesh into small pieces.

4. While the pulses, aubergine and squash are cooking, heat the ghee or oil in a casserole dish or karahi and fry the onion, garlic and ginger for 5 minutes, or until lightly brown and softened. Add the lamb and brown for 10 minutes, or until aromatic. Add the cinnamon, cardamom pods, cloves, coriander, turmeric and chilli powder and fry for 5 minutes to allow the flavours to develop. Add 170 ml (5½ fl oz/⅔ cup) water, cover and simmer for 40 minutes, or until the lamb is tender.

5. Add the mashed lentils and all the cooked and raw vegetables to the pan. Add the lime juice and simmer for 15 minutes (if the sauce is too thick, add a little water). Stir well, then check the seasoning. The dhansak should be flavoursome, aromatic, tart and spicy.

Musaman beef curry

SERVES 4 ❋ PREPARATION TIME: 15 MINUTES ❋ COOKING TIME: 1½ HOURS

This rich, creamy curry is a classic among Thai curries. Its origins are unclear but today it is mainly associated with the southern, Muslim areas of Thailand. Complex with sweet and sour spices, it is unusual in that it also incorporates a starchy ingredient such as potatoes.

1 tablespoon tamarind pulp
2 tablespoons oil
750 g (1 lb 10 oz) lean stewing
   beef, cubed
500 ml (17 fl oz/2 cups)
   coconut milk
4 cardamom pods, bruised
500 ml (17 fl oz/2 cups) coconut
   cream (do not shake the tins)
2–3 tablespoons ready-made
   musaman curry paste
8 baby onions
8 baby potatoes, cut in half if
   too large
2 tablespoons fish sauce
2 tablespoons shaved palm sugar
   (jaggery)
70 g (2½ oz/½ cup) unsalted
   roasted ground peanuts
coriander (cilantro) leaves to serve

Note: Tamarind pulp is available from Asian grocers, Thai grocers and supermarkets.

1. Put the tamarind pulp and 125 ml (4 fl oz/½ cup) boiling water in a bowl and set aside to cool. When cool, mash the pulp to dissolve in the water, then strain and reserve the liquid. Discard the pulp.

2. Heat the oil in a wok or a large saucepan and cook the beef in batches over high heat for 5 minutes, or until browned. Reduce the heat and add the coconut milk and cardamom, and simmer for 1 hour, or until the beef is tender. Add the potatoes for the final 25 minutes of cooking. Remove the beef, strain and reserve the beef and cooking liquid.

3. While the beef is cooking, put the thick coconut cream from the top of the tins in a saucepan, bring to a rapid simmer over medium heat, stirring occasionally, and cook for 5–10 minutes, or until the mixture 'splits' (the oil starts to separate). Add the curry paste and onion cook for 5 minutes, or until paste becomes aromatic and onions soften. Add the beef mixture, fish sauce, palm sugar, peanuts and tamarind liquid, and simmer for 5–10 minutes. Garnish with fresh coriander leaves.

Pour boiling water onto the tamarind pulp to soften it.

Strain the mashed pulp to obtain the tamarind liquid.

10 mins

Pork vindaloo

SERVES 4 * PREPARATION TIME: 10 MINUTES * COOKING TIME: 1¾ HOURS

The Portuguese first introduced this pork, garlic and vinegar stew to Goa. The locals adopted it but, finding it lacking slightly in flavour, proceeded to adapt it, adding spices, extra garlic and a hefty quantity of chillies. The result is vindaloo, famed — or feared — for its heat and spiciness

1 kg (2 lb 4 oz) pork fillet
3 tablespoons oil
2 onions, finely chopped
4 garlic cloves, crushed
1 tablespoon finely chopped ginger
1 tablespoon garam masala
2 teaspoons brown mustard seeds
4 tablespoons ready-made
   vindaloo paste

1. Trim the pork fillet of any excess fat and sinew and cut into bite-sized pieces.

2. Heat the oil in a saucepan, add the meat in small batches and cook over medium heat for 5–7 minutes, or until browned. Remove from the pan.

3. Add the onion, garlic, ginger, garam masala and mustard seeds to the pan, and cook, stirring, for 5 minutes, or until the onion is soft.

4. Return all the meat to the pan, add the vindaloo paste and cook, stirring, for 2 minutes. Add 625 ml (21½ fl oz/2½ cups) water and bring to the boil. Reduce the heat and simmer, covered, for 1½ hours, or until the meat is tender.

mustard seeds

There are three main varieties of mustard seeds: black, the hottest and most pungent; brown; and white (sometimes called yellow). Mustard has been cultivated for thousands of years and is eaten today in various forms all over the world. In India, in particular, mustard is considered an auspicious ingredient. Whole mustard seeds have little scent — it is only when mixed with a liquid such as water that the seeds release their distinctive aroma and sharp, biting flavour. When fried in oil until they pop, as is common in Indian curry preparations, the seeds take on a nutty taste without the searing heat. Mustard seeds are also available as a paste, powder and oil.

Beef and mustard
seed curry

SERVES 6 * PREPARATION TIME: 10 MINUTES * COOKING TIME: 2 HOURS

This comforting curry looks after itself once the initial frying of the spices is done. Stay close while cooking the spices to ensure that they do not burn. The mustard seeds, in particular, give this dish a distinctive flavour — heating them until they pop brings out their pleasant nutty taste.

3 tablespoons oil
2 tablespoons brown mustard seeds
4 dried red chillies
1 tablespoon yellow split peas
200 g (7 oz) French shallots,
  finely sliced
8 garlic cloves, crushed
1 tablespoons finely grated ginger
15 curry leaves
½ teaspoon ground turmeric
420 g (15 oz) tinned tomatoes,
  chopped
1 kg (2 lb 4 oz) braising (casserole)
  steak, diced
435 ml (15¼ fl oz/1¾ cups)
  beef stock

1. Put the oil in a heavy-based saucepan over medium heat, add the mustard seeds, chillies and split peas. As soon as the mustard seeds start to pop, add the shallots, garlic, ginger, curry leaves and turmeric. Cook for 5 minutes, then add the tomatoes, beef and stock.

2. Bring to the boil then reduce to a simmer, cover and cook for 1¾ hours, or until the beef is very tender and the sauce reduced. While cooking, skim any oil that comes to the surface and discard.

curry leaves

Shiny, dark green curry leaves are from a tropical evergreen tree native to Sri Lanka and India. The tree is a relative of the lemon tree, and shares its lingering citrusy, slightly spicy aroma. Fresh curry leaves are used widely in southern Indian, Sri Lankan and Malay cooking. When added whole to dishes, the leaves are first cooked in oil to extract their aroma and distinct flavour, then discarded at the end and not eaten. They are also used as a garnish. Fresh leaves should be kept in the refrigerator. If buying dried leaves, choose ones that have retained their green colour.

index

A READER'S DIGEST BOOK

Published by The Reader's Digest Association Limited
11 Westferry Circus
Canary Wharf
London E14 4HE
www.readersdigest.co.uk

We are committed to both the quality of our products and the service we
provide to our customers. We value your comments, so please feel free to
call us on 08705 113366, or via our website at www.readersdigest.co.uk.
If you have any comments about the content of any of your books, you can
contact us at bgeditorial@readersdigest.co.uk

This book was designed, edited and produced by Murdoch Books Pty Limited.

Series Food Editor: Fiona Roberts
Designer: Joanna Byrne
Design Concept: Uber Creative
Production: Kita George

Printed by Midas Printing (Asia) Ltd. PRINTED IN CHINA.

IMPORTANT: Those who might be at risk from the effects of salmonella
poisoning (the elderly, pregnant women, young children and those suffering
from immune deficiency diseases) should consult their doctor with any
concerns about eating raw eggs.

CONVERSION GUIDE: You may find cooking times vary depending on the
oven you are using. For fan-assisted ovens, as a general rule, set the oven
temperature to 20°C (35°F) lower than indicated in the recipe. We have used
20 ml (4 teaspoon) tablespoon measures. If you are using a 15 ml (3 teaspoon)
tablespoon for most recipes the difference will not be noticeable.

Book code: 410-705 UP0000-1
ISBN: 978 0 276 44252 0
Oracle code: 250011415H

You can order spices and seasonings online from:
www.seasonedpioneers.co.uk